WHEN THE

ROLL

IS CALLED

A PYONDER

WHEN THE ROLL

IS CALLED

A PYONDER

TALES FROM A MENNONITE CHILDHOOD

DIANA R. ZIMMERMAN

eLectio Publishing

Little Elm, TX

www.eLectioPublishing.com

When the Roll is Called A Pyonder: Tales from a Mennonite Childhood

By Diana R. Zimmerman

Copyright 2014 by Diana R. Zimmerman

Cover Design by eLectio Publishing, LLC

ISBN-13: 978-1-63213-046-4

Published by eLectio Publishing, LLC

Little Elm, Texas

http://www.eLectioPublishing.com

Printed in the United States of America

Publisher's Note

This book is dedicated to

my parents
who steered me with love through the adventures of a
happy childhood

and to my sisters
who have grown up to be my
best friends.

The author, Janey and Hoppy.
The kitchen floor, 1972.

FOREWORD

This is the memoir of a childhood in the 1970s on a Mennonite family farm in Lancaster County, Pennsylvania. It begins where my first hazy memories dawn—in the spring of the year my parents purchased and moved to the farm where they would raise my sisters and me. Through it unfolds an indecipherable mix of the real and the imagined: a family, a faith, dogs and cats, and the antics of growing children as our minds are being shaped to fit inside the world as it has been prescribed for us.

The Mennonite community in Lancaster took root in the days when the states were still colonies, when William Penn, founder of Pennsylvania, opened his territories to Swiss and German immigrant Mennonites who were escaping persecution at the hands of the protestant church in the Old World. They crossed the Atlantic in search of a land where they could practice their religion without fear. One of the displaced noblemen to purchase to a large tract of land from Penn was Christian Brubaker, my maternal grandfather 11 generations removed. His descendants farmed that same land for 200 years, until the city of Lancaster that was once a crossroads enveloped and swallowed it. I am a child of the last generation to remember the original farmstead as "grandma's house."

Mennonite tradition emphasizes the importance of being "different from the (rest of the) world," and from the time of my earliest memories I have been aware, on some level, of a split between "us" (the Mennonites) and "them" (everyone else). I realized the uniqueness of the dichotomized universe I was born into only as I became old enough to leave it. I puzzled long over how to tell these simple stories, finally settling upon letting *the child* tell them in her own voice, in the way that she experiences them.

The story ends on the day that my mother gives me the thin red notebook that will become my first diary, a day between my 10th birthday and the start of spring. All of this is the forward to the book of my life that is still being written.

PART ONE

HUNTING BUNNIES

D addy holds me up where I can see the big cows. It's dark in the barn and the steers are huffing through their noses and pushing each other. I hold on tight because they are looking at me with their big watery eyes and I don't want Daddy to put me down.

Outside in the sunshine we can look at them over the fence. They walk in the mud and chew with their tongues going in and out. Outside in the sunshine I am not scared and Daddy helps me stand on the fence and hold on.

There is a hole in the bathroom floor and I have to be careful or I could fall in. Daddy is fixing it and I want to watch.

Daddy says, "Be careful," and I am careful. The floor is broken and you can look at the broken wood and the dark underneath it.

My leg goes in the hole and I scream because I'm going to fall in and go all the way under the bathroom into the cellar.

Daddy tells me I'm ok and asks me to be careful again. I don't want to watch anymore.

At our house, we have doggies. Jack is our daddy dog. Playgo is the mommy. They're beagle dogs that Daddy goes hunting with. Playgo has puppies. She lies on the porch and I pet her. I like her. Her nipples have milk for her babies.

I lie on the porch beside Playgo. I bite her nipple like a puppy. Playgo bites me. She doesn't bite me very hard, but I cry because she scared me. Mommy runs outside and says, "What Did You Do?"

I say, "Nothing. Playgo bit me."

Mommy knows I did something because Playgo doesn't bite.

We have kitties too. Some kitties are wild and live in the barn. Daddy throws them dead chickens from the chicken house. Other kitties are tame and eat kitty food on the porch. I love kitties. I hold them by the head like my dollies. They scratch me.

Daddy and Mommy tell me, "NO!" They make me say it:

> *Not by the ears,*
> *Not by the tail,*
> *Not by the fuzzies,*
> *But by the BELLY.*

One day I put a pinchy clothespin on the tail of a kitty to see what it does. It meows at me and runs away before I can take it off. It never comes back, ever. I think it runs around the whole world and no one can ever catch it to take the clothespin off.

That wasn't nice of me. I feel sad about that.

In the bathroom is a wash basket full of washcloths and in the basket a black kitty is sitting. The washcloths are all bright colors and the black kitty is looking at me. Its eyes are yellow and it sees me.

But then I'm in my bed and we don't have that many washcloths and no kitties are allowed in the house. Mommy says that's a dream. I want the black kitty, but it isn't there.

I go to sleep in my own room. I can look over the end of my crib through the doorway into Baby Kelly's room and see her crib. I have Peter Rabbit bunny curtains. Mommy made them. The walls are green and the floor has green and yellow linoleum. Two windows look out over the front porch at the pond. The back yard and the cornfields are out my other window.

Kelly's room has two front-porch windows too, but it's darker. It's blue and has a dark rug, and the curtains Mommy made her have big purple flowers. I love my bunny curtains.

There's a green wooden rocking chair in Kelly's room. It has flowers painted on it. Sometimes at night Mommy rocks us and sings. She sings *Jesus Loves Me* and *Jesus Loves the Little Children* and *The Lord's My Shepherd* and *Dare to Be a Daniel* and *I Know the Lord Will Make a Way for Me* and *It Is Well with My Soul* and *I Come to the Garden Alone* and *A Wonderful Savior Is Jesus My Lord*. I don't like that one too much. It scares me. It's about Jesus hiding and a cleft of a rock and shadows and a dry, thirsty land and covers me there with his hand. Mommy says cleft is like a crack in a steep mountain. That song makes me sad. It makes me think of a thirsty desert and shadows and broken mountains. I don't want Jesus to be lost in the desert in the cracked mountains. I wish she wouldn't sing that one.

My Daddy goes deer hunting. He goes hunting for bunnies and pheasants with Playgo and Fancy. I have a bunny named Hoppy. He's pink and I ride him. Hoppy can't hop; he's plastic and he has wheels. I want a real bunny. They're fuzzy and nice. I don't want to shoot bunnies like my Daddy does, I want to catch one.

I have a good idea about Hoppy. Daddy looks in the field for bunnies. I can look in the field for bunnies too. Bunnies are scared of me because I'm a girl, but bunnies aren't scared of other bunnies. Hoppy is a bunny. I can take Hoppy. When the bunnies see another bunny with me, they'll know I'm nice. They'll know I won't hurt them. I think they'll hop up to me and Hoppy.

I take Hoppy outside when Mommy isn't looking. Mommy won't understand about the nice bunnies. She'll say, "No, Honey" to me. I hold him by the handle on his head and pull him across the yard. I pull him over the dug-up dirt in the garden. It's hard to walk. I'm looking for bunnies, being really quiet. Daddy says you have to be quiet. I'm walking with Hoppy over the bumpy brown cornfield and looking around.

Then I see Mommy walking up to the garden.

"Diana, what are you doing?" she says to me.

"I'm hunting bunnies," I tell her.

Sometimes I have bad dreams. That's the only time I can sleep in Mommy and Daddy's bed. We always have to wake up Mommy if something happens like we have a bad dream or a wet bed or if we throw up. I say, "Mommy, I had a bad dream," and I push on her arm and her eyes open. She opens up the covers and makes room for me in there in the warm. I tell her what I dreamed and she says not to think about it anymore, to think about good things and ask Jesus to help me have good dreams. I don't know why Jesus sometimes forgets. Sometimes she says a prayer for me. Then when I'm sleeping she wakes up Daddy and Daddy carries me back to my bed and puts me in. I like it when Daddy carries me. Sometimes, if I have a bad dream, Mommy or Daddy comes to my room with me and lays on my floor beside me until I go back to sleep.

The other time Daddy carries us is if we go to Grandma's house and we fall asleep in the car. Or sometimes we go to a church program at night. I think I'm floating. I wake up and I'm going up the stairs with my head on Daddy's shoulder. I float through the bathroom. Daddy takes my dress off like a dolly and puts my jammies on and covers me up. Sometimes I wake up when the car stops outside the house, but I pretend I'm still sleeping so Daddy will carry me.

I save Baby Kelly and Mommy and the house from burning up. I'm in the kitchen coloring on paper and Baby Kelly is sleeping and Mommy isn't with me. There's clothes in the drier. I smell a funny smell and I look up at the air. It's full of funny little white smoke curls that look like macaroni. I heard stories on Children's Bible Hour about good children who obey Jesus and help to save their mothers and baby sisters.

I holler for Mommy. She comes fast and turns off the dryer that's making white smoke. It's good I was in the kitchen coloring so the house didn't burn down.

Outside the house, there's a little hole in the ground. It's a snake house. I see him. He's black and he's called a Blacksnake. I like him. He looks like a big worm. Daddy says he's a good snake, but Mommy gets really mad when I try to pet him. She's scared of him, but I'm not. He's scared of me and slides away.

Outside the house are also some big flowers that are pink and white. They're my favorite flowers because they're so big and soft and cool and they smell like perfume. But I'm embarrassed about them because their name sounds like "panties."

In the summer, it's not dark yet when I have to go to bed. My bunny curtains look yellow and there's a fan in the window because it's hot. I hear the peepers and I go to sleep. Then I wake up and it's dark and there's a sad, terrible moaning noise. I'm scared and I wake up Mommy. She says it's the bullfrogs in the pond singing just the way peepers sing in the grass and birds sing in the trees.

I don't really understand about the frogs. It doesn't sound like singing to me—it sounds more like crying. Frogs in stories are happy. They hop and swim. These frogs sound sad and kind of scary.

I see the face of Satan on my wall and I scream. Daddy and Mommy come over into my room and they hold me and say prayers for me but I'm still scared. His face was on the wall at the foot of my bed. Mommy and Daddy say it wasn't really Satan, it was just some funny shadows and I shouldn't be scared. They tell me Jesus is taking care of me and Jesus is stronger than Satan. They tell me to ask Jesus to help me not to imagine scary things.

I'm still scared. Satan was in my room looking at me. Daddy sleeps on my floor with me all night.

After that, we turn my bed around so I can't see that wall anymore. I guess Satan could still look at me but at least I won't be able to see him. And Jesus is watching over me and He can make Satan go away.

In Mommy and Daddy's bedroom there is a closet. Mommy's dresses are in it and Daddy's Sunday shirts and pants. The closet has steps in it where Mommy and Daddy put their shoes. The steps go up behind the pants and dresses and there's also things on them like shoe boxes and bags of clothes that don't fit us anymore. I can't go in there because Mommy says "No." I want to go in and crawl up the steps and see where they go. Mommy says, "They don't go anywhere."

But they *do* go somewhere. They go *up*. Mommy says they probably used to go up to the attic, but they got old and now we have different steps in the bathroom up to the attic. You can't have steps that don't go anywhere. I want to go up them and see where they go, but Mommy won't let me so I never can.

Grandma Brubaker is the mommy of Mommy. Grandpa Brubaker is her daddy. They have a big white house and steers and Lassie. They have a cuckoo clock where a bird jumps out of little doors and says, "*Koo-Koo, Koo-Koo!*" It's in the family room behind Grandma's chair. Grandpa has a chair too and his is yellow.

On Easter, we go to their house for dinner after church. Grandma has an Easter basket for me and she hides it. I find it behind Grandpa's chair and everyone thinks I'm a smart little girl. I am. It has funny plastic straw in it and it's all bright colors and has bright plastic eggs in it and a lot of candy. It's all for me and I can take it home but then when the candy's all gone Mommy has to give it back to Grandma for next year. It's a little different than Christmas.

Kelly gets into trouble for being naughty. We can't color on anything in the house except paper but Kelly doesn't listen. She goes upstairs and colors on the wall. She makes a giant circle on the bedroom wall with some little squiggles inside it. She tells Mommy it's Jonah and the whale.

Kelly gets in trouble for that but when I hear Mommy telling Grandma about it on the telephone, and Aunt Judy and Aunt Lucy, she doesn't sound very mad. She sounds like she thinks it's funny.

I go to the potty in the big potty but Kelly has a little potty chair. After she goes potty Mommy pulls the little dish out of it and dumps it in the big potty and flushes it down. The potty chair is only for Kelly because she's too little for the big potty. She might fall in. I'm a big girl so the potty chair isn't for me.

One day I go potty in the potty chair anyway just to try it. Mommy's very surprised to find a poop in the potty chair. She says, "Did Kelly do this?"

I say, "Yes."

I don't think she believes me.

Mommy's busy so she doesn't see me go upstairs. I have a good idea. My bureau is really big. It's so big I can't see the mirror on it unless I stand on my bed. I'm sure that if I can climb up on top of my bureau and jump, I'll be able to fly around the room like a bird. It's hard to climb up there and I have to be quiet or Mommy will find me and I'll have to sit on a chair. I get up there and I look around and my head is almost on the ceiling. I jump as high as I can.

I sink straight through the air and I bang my mouth on my bed and I bump my arms and legs and make a loud crashing noise on the floor. I cry really loud.

Mommy comes running up the stairs to see what I did. I don't want to tell her. She already told me people can't fly, but I didn't think she ever tried to.

Outside we have a washhouse. The washhouse is cool and dark. The freezer is in there, and Mommy's garden things. Mommy is busy and I have a surprise for her. I put water in a bucket and I find a scrub brush under the sink. I got to the washhouse and I wash the floor for Mommy. Mommy works very hard and washes the floor inside the house, but she never has time to wash the washhouse. This is going to be a good surprise because the washhouse is very dirty.

Mommy finds me on the floor with all the dirty water and says, "Oh, Diana! What are you doing?"

I say, "I'm washing the floor for you."

Mommy says, "Oh, Sweetie! Thank you so much, but we don't have to wash this floor. It's very dirty. We can just sweep this one."

I can tell Mommy is very surprised and she is happy I was helping all by myself. But it's true the floor is very dirty and it might be better just to sweep it.

I like to help Daddy oil his gun. Daddy goes hunting for deers and ducks and bunnies and pheasants. You have to clean guns and oil them so they work. You have to be very careful there aren't any bullets in them when you aren't outside hunting. You must never point them at a person. You must never even point a pretend gun at a person or pretend to shoot someone. That's naughty.

Daddy has a special oil rag and a little can of oil that's red and white and has a little point. It smells good. Daddy sits on the floor of the living room with me and his gun and pours on some drops of oil. He lets me rub it with the rag. I'm a good helper.

Mommy and Daddy go to a seminar. It's kind of like church where you listen to a preacher, but children don't have to go, so me and Kelly go to sleep at Grandma Brubaker's house. Before bed, we have a snack and Grandma gives me chocolate pudding.

In the middle of the night, my belly hurts and I throw up. I throw up again. I throw up again. Grandma says I have a virus, but I know it's the chocolate pudding. I'm never going to eat chocolate pudding ever ever again because it makes me throw up.

I'm a very special little girl because I can run faster than a truck. I can run as fast as the wind. Feed trucks and chicken trucks come in and go out the lane. They're tractor-trailer trucks and they make a lot of noise. You have to watch out for them because they could run over you and then you die.

I'm playing in the grass beside the lane and then there's a big truck coming up to me. I jump up and run. I look behind me and the driver doesn't stop the truck, it keeps coming toward me. I'm running as fast as I can and the truck is driving behind me, but he doesn't run over me because I'm running so fast. I'm running faster than the feed truck. I'm running as fast as the wind.

I tell Mommy what I did because I think she will be happy and feel better that she doesn't have to worry about a truck running over me. She isn't happy. She says trucks are very dangerous and I must never never run in front of them. But I'm not scared anymore now that I know how fast I can run. If I ever see one coming toward me, I can just run away.

Grandma Zimmerman's house is big and quiet. I have to take a nap even if I'm not sleepy. She takes me upstairs and puts me in a crib. It's dark brown like Kelly's crib at home. This is Aunt Barbie's bedroom but Aunt Barbie doesn't live here anymore. The room is green and cool and Grandma pulls down the blinds so the sun won't shine in so much. The blinds have little round circles hanging from them that Grandma pulls on. The circles have string wound around them. I like blinds.

There's a door to the bathroom and it isn't closed. I don't like that bathroom because the bathtub isn't attached to the floor like ours—it has feet. The feet are real. They're lions' feet. They have claws and I'm scared of them. The bathtub is a lion and I'm scared of it and I can't go to sleep until Grandma comes and closes the door to the bathroom.

I'm scared of something in Grandma Brubaker's house too. The coat hooks are deer's feet. When you go upstairs, you can't really see them but when you come down, they're sticking out of the wall at the bottom of the steps. I don't like the cut-off deer feet. Mommy says the deers were already dead when they got their feet cut off and the deer feet can't hurt me. I don't like them. I call for Mommy to come up and get me.

Sunday is for going to church. We wear Sunday dresses and Sunday shoes and Sunday coats if it's cold. Mommy puts on perfume and Daddy puts on smell-me-good.

First we have Sunday school and then we have church. Sunday school is fun because it's for children. Irene Nolt tells us Bible stories and sticks pictures of Jesus and Moses on a fuzzy cloth. We get stars by our names on the attendance chart each time we go. I have a lot of stars. At the end, we sing *Dropping, Dropping* and put the pennies our daddies gave us in the basket. Jesus likes that because people take that money and buy food for hungry children in other countries. Then we eat pretzels and drink little paper cups of juice.

After Sunday school is church. Church takes a long, long time. The preacher talks about God to the grown-ups and the children have to sit still and be quiet. Sometimes I'm sleepy and Mommy or Daddy holds me on their lap. Mommy's shoulder is littler than Daddy's and you can feel the bones under your head. Daddy is so big my head doesn't reach up to his shoulder, I just have to put my ear on his shirt and I can listen to his heart.

After church, I stand up on the bench and look for The Candy Lady. Mommy says her name is Emily and it isn't nice to call her The Candy Lady and it isn't nice to ask people for candy. But her name *is* The Candy Lady and I *know* she has candy. If she didn't like giving candy to children, she wouldn't bring a pocketbook full of it to church.

I don't know what a Pyonder is. We have a song we sing in church about *When The Roll Is Called A Pyonder I'll Be There*. A roll is sometimes called a bun, but I never heard anyone call it a pyonder. Or there are rolls like toilet paper rolls or rolls like rolling down the hill and I don't know which one you'd call a Pyonder. It's kind of a funny song. But I know it's about Jesus coming back and I know we have to be ready for that any minute.

Mommy sometimes lets me and Kelly help her wash the dishes. She fills up the yellow dishpan with water and soap and puts the stool there because we can't reach without a stool, or even see up there. We have to take turns.

I swoosh the dirty cups and plates around in the clean water with the dishcloth. Mommy washes them right because she's the mommy. Mommy is big and fast and she grabs the dishes and cups and spoons one after the other and scrubs them hard and dips them into the clean rinse water and clunks them into the dish drainer on the other side. Mommy doesn't slosh or splash or play or pretend. Mommy is busy. She's working, and when we slop too much or get in the way she says, "Ok, that's enough," and puts us on the floor and moves the stool away.

Mommy and Daddy play with us after supper, but they never play with us after dinner. After dinner, they quick have to work more.

After dinner, we can play a little and then it's naptime. I don't like naptime because I'm not sleepy and I want to keep playing. I sleep all night so I don't see why I have to sleep in the day too. I have to go lie in bed and stay there. I can't get out of bed and play upstairs. If I do, Mommy finds me and I'm in big trouble. I'm not allowed to go ask Mommy if I can get up yet, either.

When it's get-up time, Mommy takes my slip that's hanging on my outside door handle and puts it inside where I can see it. I have to wait for that. Sometimes I see Mommy's hand come around and quietly put my slip on the inside. Other times I look and it's just there.

Outside in the yard we have swings. Daddy made them. There's one for me and one for Kelly. Mine's higher than hers because I'm bigger. Daddy says, "Hold on tight," and I hold on tight. He pushes me high. The green tree leaves get close to me and I smell them and then I can only see the top of the swing set and the sky. Then I go backwards and look down at the grass. My dress has flowers on it and the grass has flowers in it. There are bees.

My favorite is when Daddy runs under the swing. Then I think I'm going to swing in a whole circle all the way around the top of the swing set. I go up past the tree and over Daddy's head and over the house and up into the sky.

I have another dream. It's a nice dream. I'm in a strange place where the walls and floors and ceilings are glass. The rooms are connected together by holes and I'm walking and jumping from room to room. Each room has something in it. One has a whale. It's like being inside a toy and I am jumping down and down through space after space, looking all around. I kind of like it there. The last hole I hop down through lands me on a chair in the middle of the living room where Mommy is having Bible study with other ladies. I'm very surprised. I remember this dream forever.

D addy has a horsey named Ringo. Ringo is brown and he's very big. Daddy rides Ringo with me. Mommy and Kelly don't ride him because Mommy's scared and Kelly's too little. Daddy catches Ringo in the meadow and puts reins and a saddle on him. Daddy climbs up on Ringo and sits on top and Mommy helps me jump up too. I sit in the front and hold on to the handle really tight so I won't fall off. Daddy holds on to me. We walk around the yard way up high on the top of Ringo's back. We jerk around funny, but I'm not scared and I say giddy-up.

Daddy gets off Ringo and I'm sitting up on the saddle holding on tight all by myself. Daddy says I'm a good cowboy and he pulls on Ringo's reins to make Ringo walk around more. I hold on, but I don't like all that jerking and wobbling when Daddy isn't holding on to me. I'm up high as the trees. I start crying for Daddy to get me down. He says, "It's ok," but it isn't ok. I want down so I cry louder and louder. I don't like it up there all by myself.

Me and Kelly get baby kitties. Daddy finds them in the barn without a mommy kitty. Our mommy doesn't like kitties in the house, but it's too cold for baby kitties to live outside so she lets them live in the cellar. My kitty is the cutest and I name him Cutie. Kelly names her kitty Andrew because Andrew is the preacher at Erismans' church. Andrew was also a disciple.

We make Cutie and Andrew wear dolly clothes. They can only wear bonnets and dresses. They can't wear panties because there's no place for their tails to come out. They don't like clothes very much and they walk out of them. They don't stay in the dolly crib or the coach either unless we hold them down.

When spring comes, the kitties are big so Mommy makes them live outside.

Andrew falls in the manure pit from the hog house and dies because he can't get out. Cutie dies later. Kitties are nice but then they always die.

There are rules about where we can play, and we can't play upstairs when Mommy is downstairs. We can only play up there on Saturdays while Mommy cleans. Another place we can't play is in the bathroom.

But the upstairs has so many exciting things. Everything up there is interesting. Downstairs are just the same old dollies and books and crayons. I get in trouble a lot for going upstairs. I cut my finger because I never imagine that the little metal squares in the medicine cabinet could be that sharp. I find a box of white paper sticks and I get in trouble for asking Mommy what they are. Mommy says they're for big ladies not little girls and I wonder what big ladies want funny white sticks and sharp metal for.

I get in trouble upstairs because I decorate a temple for King Solomon. We learn about it in Sunday school, and the picture in the Sunday school book shows great columns of gold, carpets and beautiful decorations. Under the sink in the upstairs bathroom is a cabinet where Mommy puts towels and toilet paper and soap. I take them out. It looks like a perfect place to make a Holy of Holies. Toilet paper is soft and delicate and beautiful. The Lord will love a toilet paper temple. I unravel it, roll after roll, preparing a dwelling place for Him. I'm on my way from the bathroom to Mommy and Daddy's bedroom unraveling a long piece behind me when Mommy comes upstairs and finds me. She doesn't think my toilet paper temple is beautiful at all. She gets all mad about the toilet paper. I don't know why—it isn't ruined. You can still tear it up later and use it.

I also get hurt for playing upstairs when I'm not supposed to. The potty is full of clean water and I like to play in water. Mommy doesn't like it and she calls it "slopping." I put the lids up and I'm slopping in the water but the seat accidentally comes back down and hits me on the head. It hits me on the forehead really hard because it's very heavy and I cry really really loud. Mommy comes upstairs and says, "What happened?"

I don't want to tell her because I was naughty and she might smack me but I'm already crying so she doesn't. Later I have a big huge bump on my head from the potty seat. It turns purple.

Me and Kelly play dollies. My dolly is Janey. Janey used to be Mommy's dolly when Mommy was little. Janey is plastic and you can make her arms and legs stick out so she sits up by herself. Her eyes go shut when you lay her down and open when you pick her up. Her mouth has a hole in it for a dolly bottle, but you can pour real water in it if you want and then she wets because there's a hole in her bottom. Mommy doesn't like that—she doesn't like us slopping in water or playing about going to the bathroom. I feed Janey raisins. She rattles forever.

Kelly's dolly's name is Thousie. Kelly made that name up out of her head. Thousie is a new dolly so she isn't all plastic like Janey— her arms and legs are, but her belly is soft. Thousie can't get wet or Mommy says she will get rotten.

Thousie and Janey get sick. They have colds. Me and Kelly take good care of them. We grease them with Vicks like Mommy does to us when we have colds.

Mommy gets very mad because we know we're not supposed to open the medicine cabinet where she keeps big-people things. She takes away the Vicks and the dollies. Janey gets washed, but she has to throw Thousie away and get Kelly a different Thousie. Mommy says she's going to put the Vicks "Away Far Over Jordan" like in the song.

I hope she can get it back when I catch a cold again.

Sometimes even children or babies die. I decide if Kelly dies I don't want Mommy and Daddy to bury her. I want them to get her stuffed like Daddy's deer heads so I can play with her. That would be nice.

Daddy makes a tire swing and puts it in the big tree in the yard. It's a car tire that hangs on a chain, but you have to be careful of the chain because it can pinch your fingers. Me and Kelly take turns swinging and pushing on it. Daddy thinks up the good idea of making holes in it because otherwise when it rains it gets full of water on the bottom and it slops all over us. We try to put kitties and puppies in it, but they jump out. They don't think it's very fun.

We have a swimming pool for summer. It's blue and plastic and Mommy puts the hose in it to make it full of water. There's a sliding board you can slide down on your bottom or your belly. You can even go down backwards. You can stand up on it and jump off and make a big splash. Grass gets in the swimming pool because of our feet. Bugs get in there too.

Me and Kelly have swimming suits. Mine is yellow and orange and it has a little skirt. It's the prettiest swimming suit in the world and I'm the prettiest little girl in the world when I go swimming.

In the winter, we have to wear coats with hoods because it's cold outside. We have to wear mittens too that Mommy clips onto the sleeves of our coats so we won't lose them. We lose them anyway.

I have a beautiful coat. It's like Joseph's Coat of Many Colors that made his brothers so jealous they wanted to kill him. Mine's not striped like Joseph's—mine's flowered—but it's just as beautiful and has even more colors. I love my winter coat. The hood has white bunny fuzz around it.

I don't know what I want to be when I grow up. I can't decide. I don't want to be a mommy like Mommy and I can't be a farmer like Daddy because I'm a girl. I think maybe I'll be a rock collector. I like rocks. I like to play in the lane and pick out pretty stones and bring them inside.

Then I see a circus on TV and I know what I want to be. I want to be an acrobat. I want to hang upside down on a flying trapeze and flip through the air. That must be the most fun thing in the world. I practice doing somersaults and standing on my head.

Rocky and Bobby come to stay at our house. They're "Fresh Air Boys," which means they live in the city and they aren't used to the country. Rocky and Bobby are black. There are a lot of black people in cities, but we don't have any here in the country. I like Rocky and Bobby, but they're bigger than me and they don't really want to play with me. They sleep in the spare room beside my room. I wish I could see what's in their suitcases, but I'm not allowed to go in there.

Rocky and Bobby are funny. They think our doggies might bite them and they don't like the kitties. Daddy tells them they can't chase the kitties. They're scared to play in the barn because they think someone might be hiding in there. But we're the only people who go into our barn. They don't like it in the chicken house because they think the chicken manure is yucky and they say it stinks. They don't know how to catch fish in the pond and they don't like worms. They want to watch TV in the daytime and Mommy and Daddy say "*No!*" and say they have to play outside. I guess some people watch TV in the day. They have to wear flip-flops outside even though it's hot because everything hurts their feet.

The funniest thing about Rocky and Bobby is that they're scared of the dark. They're big boys and they're scared of the dark! They won't even go out into the yard and catch lightning bugs. I feel kind of sorry for them.

We go to The Mennonite Home to see Great Grandma and Grandpa Neff. Those are Grandma's mommy and daddy. I don't think Grandma really needs a mommy and daddy—she's Grandma. When Grandma was a little girl, Great Grandma and Grandpa Neff weren't that old and they lived in a house and they could walk.

It's kind of dark in their room and we have to be quiet. They aren't sick, but we have to be quiet anyway and behave. We always wear Sunday dresses. Great Grandpa sits in a big recliner with a zig-zaggy knitted blanket over his legs. He does that even when it isn't cold. He has a metal box called a walker to walk in when he has to go to the bathroom. Great Grandma only has a cane. They have a light on a little table and if you wait for it to get warmed up, red blobs float around in the yellow water. I like it.

Grandpa Zimmerman doesn't have any hairs on his head. That's because he's old. I'm at Grandpa's house and Grandma is making dinner and Grandpa is holding me on his lap. He's twisting the handle of a box that sings music and then a clown jumps out. It's funny. It wiggles like it's surprised like I am. I ask Grandpa what happened to his hair. He says Grandma pulled it out. Grandma laughs. I don't think it's too funny. That's not very nice. Me and Kelly pull each other's hair and it hurts. Then we get into trouble. I can't understand why Grandma pulled out Grandpa's hair. Maybe she didn't really do it.

In the car, we have sides and we have to stay on them. My side is behind Mommy and Kelly's side is behind Daddy. When we go to Grandma Brubaker's house, we have to drive past a big hole called a stone quarry where they dig up stones to put on the lane. There's a fence around it, but it's on my side and it's so big we could fall in. It's so deep the rain and snow don't fill it up. I don't like the stone quarry. I'm scared of such a big hole. I think we could fall in with the car.

Sometimes when we come home late at night me and Kelly play a game in the car. We call it "Playing Our Violins," but it's not real because we don't have violins and if we did, Mommy wouldn't let us play them in the car. Me and Kelly sit down on the floor behind the seats. There's a hump in the middle. Down there, we sing all the songs we can think of and that's how we Play Our Violins.

Other times we get sleepy and then one girl can lie down on the seat and the other girl gets to lie on the back window. My favorite is lying on the back window even when it's cold, but Mommy and Daddy make us take turns. I look up at the stars and the moon if it's out and watch all the lights zooming by around the bottom of the sky. I watch everything turn sideways when we go around a corner. I guess when I get big I won't fit on the back window anymore, which is too bad because I like it there.

Kelly tells me she has to go into the sewing room all by herself because she can open her head up in there and get out a good idea. I don't think that's true. People can't open up their heads. She says, "Yuh-huh, I can so," but she won't let me watch.

I wait in the living room. Me and Kelly like to do plays we make up and we want to make a new one. There's one play called Mr. Marshmallow and I get to be Mr. Marshmallow. I have to sit on the piano bench and scrunch my knees up and hold them so I look like a marshmallow. Then I have to roll off and fall on the floor.

When Kelly comes out of the sewing room, she has a good idea. I don't think she opened her head up, though.

Me and Kelly are laughing really hard and Mommy says, "What are you girls, The Silly Committee?" Me and Kelly think that's funny and we laugh even more. Mommy says if we want to be that silly, we have to go play in the cellar. So me and Kelly go down into the cellar where we have the little red wagon and the floor is cement and there are jars of canned things Mommy made and Daddy's old ice skates and the furnace. We jump around and squeal and make funny faces and funny noises and say, "HAHAHAHA!" so loud we make ourselves laugh for real. This is how we have Silly Committee. It's a fun game, but we always have to play it in the cellar. If the Silly Committee gets too noisy, Mommy comes down and makes us stop it.

Grandma Zimmerman comes to help Mommy do peas. They're very busy working. It's hot and I want to go swimming. Mommy says, "No."

We have baby kitties. They're hot too because they're fuzzy, but they're afraid of the water because kitties can't swim. Doggies can swim and kitties can't. I think if the kitties could swim, they wouldn't be afraid. That would be nice. Then they could swim with us in the pool.

I have a good idea. I take the kitties down to the pond. I'm going to teach them how to swim and then maybe when they grow up and have babies they can teach them to swim too. I'm not allowed to play in the pond but Mommy isn't looking and I'm only going to stand in it with my feet.

The kitties don't like it. They meow and scratch. But they're just babies and they don't know I'm helping them. After they learn to swim, they won't meow and scratch anymore. The kitties are all wet. My dress is all wet. They stop scratching, but they aren't trying to swim like I'm showing them.

Mommy comes up behind me and gets me and she is very mad. She's mad because I'm all wet and the kitties are all wet and I disobeyed. She says I was drowning the kitties and I was not. I was helping them. She says, "Kitties don't need help," and she makes me go up to the house and Mommy spanks me and Grandma sees I was a bad girl. I have to change my wet dress.

I don't want to go downstairs to see Grandma. I don't want to play. I wasn't drowning the kitties.

Me and Kelly and Kristen play church. We take our dollies and sit on the steps at Grandma's house. The dollies have to be quiet. We feed them bottles of milk from our diaper bags.

Kristen smacks and pinches. She pulls our hair. Her mommy is Aunt Judy. If I smack her back or pull her hair she starts to cry and then Mommy smacks me because you're not supposed to smack. I run and tell Aunt Judy when Kristen is being mean. Aunt Judy says, "Kristen Ann Stevens," and Mommy says it isn't nice to be a tattletale. Mommy says Kristen is just little and she's still learning.

I don't think she's learning anything because she keeps doing it. And it hurts a lot when she pinches me.

Daddy plants corn in the fields. He plants field corn, which is different than the corn on the cob Mommy puts in the garden. You can't eat field corn. Field corn is for making things like chicken feed and pig feed and cow feed. You could make something like Corn Flakes out of it and then you could eat it.

The seed corns are pink, which is funny because corn is yellow. Daddy says that's because they have fertilizer on them and you shouldn't touch them because it's bad for you. But I like the pretty pink corns.

When it's time to plant corn Daddy gets a special thing for behind the tractor that isn't like the disk or the plow. He drives up and down the fields and the corns come out and fall into the dirt. Then they grow up bigger and bigger until they're bigger than Daddy and you can't see the line fence anymore. After they're done growing they dry up and turn brown because it's Fall. They look all dead but they're not. They're really ready for the corn pickers.

That's when Abner Brant comes. Abner Brant knows Grandpa too. Abner is a funny name. He brings his harvester to our farm to pick the corn for Daddy because Daddy doesn't have a harvester and that's the way you have to pick field corn. The harvester is like a tractor, but it's so big you can see it all the way at the end of the line fence.

Abner comes in for dinner and supper with Daddy and they're hot and tired and they don't want to talk to little girls. It's dark outside when I go to bed and I can see the lights on the harvester out there picking corn in the dark. Abner has to hurry up and work in the dark because Daddy doesn't want it to rain.

M e and Kelly get into fights. I hate her. I wish she were dead. Sometimes people kill each other but I don't have anything to kill Kelly with. Besides, killing people is a sin and I would go to hell. But I could just tell Jesus I was sorry and he'd have to forgive me because Jesus forgives everyone. He forgives other people who kill people.

I remember the story of David and Goliath and how little David kills the giant Goliath with a slingshot and a stone. I don't have a slingshot. I don't really know what a slingshot is but in the story David swings it really fast around and around, and the stone flies out and hits Goliath on the head and he dies. I don't think it hurts too much. If it could kill a giant like Goliath, it ought to work on Kelly. And we have lots of stones.

I find a dolly bonnet with strings on it and I get some stones. Mommy is outside working and Kelly is playing on the porch. I put a stone in the dolly bonnet and hide behind the washer. I wait for Kelly to walk past the doorway so I can sling my sling 'round and 'round like in the song. I imagine Kelly lying on the ground with a red star on her forehead like Goliath.

Mommy and Daddy will have a fit if Kelly dies. I could say I didn't try it, but they will still have a fit. I'll get spanked for sure. They love her a lot and they'll cry and then we'll have to bury her. I decide not to kill her after all.

The Stick is on top of the refrigerator. It used to be a yardstick, but it broke and now it's The Stick. It's old and green. If Mommy or Daddy reaches up on top of the refrigerator and gets The Stick, somebody is going to get spanked and it's usually me. I start to cry when I see The Stick because they never change their minds about it. If you even see The Stick, you might as well start crying awhile. Sometimes Daddy spanks us without The Stick, just with his hand, but The Stick is sharper. They sit down and stand us against their legs and bend us over and smack our bottoms with The Stick. This is what happens if we're mean or bad or back talk or don't listen. I don't want to cry when Mommy and Daddy spank me. I want to say that didn't hurt, but it hurts a lot and I cry a lot.

Daddy spanks me with The Stick and then when I'm crying he sits on the rocking chair and picks me up onto his lap and gives me his hanky and rocks me. He says he loves me and that's why he has to spank me—so I will learn to obey him like God wants children to obey their parents. I already know that. I want to be a good girl and I cry more because I was bad.

I can only cry for a little bit though because if I keep crying and crying because I'm mad at him, Daddy says, "Now, it's time to stop crying, or I'll give you something to cry about." That means you're about to get spanked again for crying too much. If you cry too much, you get spanked again and then you cry more because it hurts and you still have to stop crying. I don't know why Mommy and Daddy spank us if they want us to be nice. Spanking isn't nice.

Sometimes we go to Grandma and Grandpa's church on Sunday. It's exciting to go to a new church. Sunday school is full of new boys and girls and the preacher isn't Marty Nolt, it's someone else. Grandma and Grandpa's church is different than ours. At theirs, the men and ladies can't sit together; they each have to stay on their own sides. Only little boys and girls are allowed to sit on the other side. I always sit with Grandpa on the men's side. I like to hear all the deep voices together when they sing. Plus, when I'm big I'm going to have to sit on the ladies' side so I might as well sit on the men's side now. Grandma's church is called Roherstown Mennonite. Ours is Erbs.

Daddy makes me a flying trapeze like in the circus out of a broom handle and he hangs it from the tree in the yard. I run and grab it and fly. I hang upside down by my knees and my hair almost swooshes on the ground. Mommy says, "You be careful," and Daddy says, "Hang on tight," and Grandma Brubaker says, "Ruthie, you better watch her."

I'm not scared at all. I'm strong and quick. I'm a good acrobat. I can "skin the cat." Not for real, though—it's a trick I learn. When you skin the cat is when you climb up onto the trapeze like a swing and you sit there but you let go of the chains and grab the bar between your legs and you fall off on purpose and your legs flip over your head and you land on the ground standing up. If you put your hands on the outside of your legs, you can do it backwards too.

Mommy takes me to visit Minnie. Minnie is so old she can only lie in bed at the old peoples' home, but she likes to talk. I like Minnie. She has a funny screechy quiet voice and her hands look like branches but they're soft like the nose of Ringo, our horsey. Minnie gives me candy. She has a lot of pretty decorations in her room. Minnie and Mommy talk about Grandma and Grandpa Brubaker and other people in the family because Minnie is in our family too, but she isn't my grandma. She's somebody else's grandma.

Minnie likes me so much she gives me a present. It's one of her decorations. She gives me a special bar of soap that smells good, covered up in a knitted orange case with pink plastic flowers on top. It's to make the clothes in your drawers smell good, she says. I love it. Minnie's going to die soon and I'm going to keep her soap forever and never take a bath with it even when it doesn't smell good anymore. I'm never going to throw it away or forget about Minnie.

Grandma Brubaker comes to our house to help Mommy do beans and peaches and corn. I sit on Grandma's lap in the kitchen while she is talking to Mommy. I see Grandma's hands and how they look. They don't look like Mommy's hands. Mommy's hands are strong and scratchy from dish soap and string beans and weeding the garden. Grandma's hands look bony and I can see right through her skin. Her veins stick out because her skin is old and sticks to them.

I remember that grandmas in storybooks are old and sometimes they die. Great Grandpa Neff was old and he died. I see Grandma's old hands and I think maybe Grandma is going to die like other old people.

I ask her, "Grandma? Are you going to die soon?"

"Ha!" Grandma shouts like a loud laugh. "By golly, I sure hope not!"

I hope not too. Anyway, she doesn't act like she's going to die soon.

Mommy makes our dresses. She makes our dolly dresses. She makes her dresses too, but she buys Daddy's clothes at K-Mart or Penny's. Mommy sews on the sewing machine and I sew too, but I can't use a real needle because they're sharp. I have to pretend. Mommy makes our jammies and our housecoats and curtains for the windows.

Mommy makes me bloomers to wear to church. She says, "Keep your legs down" and "Keep your dress down" and "Sit nice" all the time, but it isn't fair. Boys can do anything they want and run and play and fall down and roll in the grass and no one can see their underwear.

After church, I run outside and play with Tommy and Johnny Martin and Darvin. There is a bar around the graveyard where the dead people are and we can do flips on it. Mommy and Daddy get mad because they say I'm showing everybody in church my panties. I don't really care. Everybody wears panties, and besides, I'm just a little girl. I won't do flips when I'm a big lady. I try to sit right, but I think I never do. Anyway, isn't that what Sunday panties are for?

Bloomers are like shorts except that we don't wear shorts. We don't believe in shorts. I wonder what it would be like to wear them. Mommy puts elastic around the legs of our bloomers and me and Kelly wear them under our dresses so no one can see our Sunday panties. She puts a little tag on the front so we don't put them on backwards. Not a wonder it takes so long to get ready for church— we have panties and bloomers and slips and dresses and shoes and socks. At home, we just wear dresses and panties and we don't care if anybody sees them.

Mommy says I have to wait till next year to go to kindergarten. I want to go now. Kindergarten is where you play and color and learn things and take a book bag to school and sing and you have a teacher like in Sunday school. I want to go to kindergarten now. Otherwise, I have to stay home for a whole year and play with Kelly. I'm big enough for kindergarten now. I can't wait for one year. I know I can't. Mommy says, "You can't go to Kindergarten until you're five," and I'm not five yet. But I'm almost five. But I can't go after my birthday either; I have to wait all the way till next year when I'm almost six. It's not fair.

We go to revival meeting at church and every night some of the big boys and girls stand up to ask Jesus into their hearts when we sing *Just As I Am*. Then their mommies and daddies hug them and cry and the preacher says that the angels in heaven are rejoicing and that the devil is sad. I want to ask Jesus into my heart too. I love Jesus because he died on the cross for my sins. I know I'm too little to stand up in church because I'd have to stand on the bench for the preacher to see me. I'm four. But I ask Jesus into my heart anyway.

When Mommy is tucking me into bed, I tell her. She says she's very happy. She says she knows I love Jesus, but I can't stand up in church until I'm bigger. Mommy says I have to wait till I'm bigger to decide I want to be a Christian and try to live like Jesus. She says children can't be members of the church at least until they're twelve.

I'm sad. I already know I want to be a Christian and follow Jesus. I did think about it already. I know I don't want to lie and steal and shoot people and listen to rock music and say bad words.

I'm a little confused now. In the Bible Jesus says, "Let the little children come to Me." I'm too little for almost everything and now I'm too little for Jesus. I didn't think you could be too little for that. I'm not too little to be good. I have to be good all the time.

At nighttime, me and Kelly sometimes get leg aches. It feels like our legs are breaking, but there's nothing wrong with them. Mommy says they're growing pains because our legs are growing so fast it makes our bones hurt. She gives us Tylenol when we say, "Mommy I have a leg ache." I don't know why things have to grow so fast they hurt you.

Mommy gets headaches, but that's different.

I have a bad dream and Mommy lets me get into bed with her while I tell her what it was. Then she says a prayer to Jesus that I won't have any more bad dreams. It wasn't that bad of a dream, I guess, because she says I have to go lie in my own bed and trust Jesus. I want to stay in here with Mommy and Daddy, but I'm getting big so sometimes they say "No."

I have to go through the dark bathroom to get to my bed and when I'm walking around the bathtub, there's somebody there. I'm still scared from my dream and I scream really loud.

The person in the dark screams back at me and it's just Kelly, but I scream again and Mommy screams too because everyone is in the dark screaming. Me and Kelly start crying and Daddy starts laughing and me and Kelly run to Mommy and Daddy and they have to let us *both* under the covers so the whole family is in one bed. Daddy says we're a bunch of crazy girls and now Mommy is laughing too but I don't think it's funny how scared I was and Kelly doesn't either.

After that Mommy buys a night light for in the bathroom so you can see if someone else is there. I don't go to sleep until it's on, ever for the rest of my life.

Mommy washes our hair on Saturdays so it will be clean for church. Me and Kelly have long hair but mine is light brown like Daddy's and hers is dark brown like Mommy's.

I don't like it when Mommy washes my hair. Sometimes I cry. She washes me with pink soap and then I have to turn around. She turns the water on and pushes me over backwards until my hair is under the spigot and my hair gets heavy and my head feels like it's going to fall off. Then I can sit up and Mommy puts shampoo onto my head. She scratches it all around with her fingers. She does it hard and it hurts. I ask Mommy does she have to do it with her fingernails. She says, "Oh, Honey, I'm not using my fingernails. I just use my fingers." Then she doesn't scratch quite as hard anymore until next time.

When it's time to rinse the shampoo out, she makes me turn around again and put my head back under the water again. I get to put a washcloth over my eyes so shampoo doesn't get in them. Water is splashing all over my face and my nose tickles and I can't see and I can't breathe. Mommy rubs out the shampoo and I have to hold my head up and I can't hold it up anymore. But if I sit up I get in trouble and if I put my head back the whole way all the water goes into my nose and mouth. I wish we could have short hair like boys, but the Bible says we can't. It's not fair, but we have to obey it.

After bath, Daddy combs us. Daddy always says our hair is pretty and it smells good like shampoo. He says, "I smell 'poo" for shampoo and we laugh because we aren't allowed to say that word. Daddy can say it though when he means *shampoo*. If Mommy hears him say it, she says, "Lamar!" and looks at him out of the top of her eyes.

In the summer, Daddy takes the blue comb and sits on the porch and combs out the tangles. I wear my Noah's Ark jammies. We listen to the peepers and Daddy tells me about animals like peepers that are really little frogs and about fish that live in the pond and bumblebees that live in nests and worms that live in the dirt. He tells me stories about when he was a little boy. In the winter we can't sit outside, we have to sit inside, and me and Daddy watch *Hee Haw* while he combs me. People on that program talk funny and they walk around in the cornfield and Miss Mimi forgets to take the tag off her hat. Mommy doesn't like *Hee Haw* and she doesn't like Daddy to watch it or us. She says it's too dumb and she tries to wash our hair during it so we can't watch.

Mommy cuts our bangs. She doesn't cut all our hair because the Bible says girls and ladies have to have long hair. But it's ok to cut your bangs so they don't get in your eyes.

I hate it when Mommy cuts my bangs. She says, "Sit still," and I sit still but she always wants me to sit *more* still. She combs my bangs right down into my eyes and nose and they tickle me and make me sneeze. Then she gets a piece of Scotch Tape and puts it on my head where she wants to cut so they won't turn out crooked. I sit still, but she says, "Sit still!" even louder and pulls off the tape and puts it on again. It hurts. Then she cuts off the piece of tape and hairs fall in my eyes and nose and mouth and on my arms and down my dress. She says, *"Sit still!"* and the big sharp, angry scissors is cutting right by my eyes making little itchies all over my face.

When she's done, I run to the mirror to see my cut-off bangs and my big eyebrows are underneath them so I look surprised.

On top of our house is the attic. The attic door is in the bathroom and we aren't allowed to go up there unless Mommy goes up and says we can come. The attic is very hot in the summer and very cold in the winter. It feels like being outside. The attic has a lot of secret things we can't see like presents Mommy bought for us that we can't have yet because it isn't Christmas. Mommy's special things are up there too like her wedding dress and extra things like special dishes that can break. Daddy has books up there and songbooks and lots of papers. Some day when I'm big I'm going to sneak up into the attic and look in the boxes. I won't break anything or take anything out—I just want to see what's in there.

Miles and Sandy are Mommy and Daddy's friends. Miles talks really loud and Sandy always thinks everything is funny. They have Sharon for me to play with and Marsha for Kelly. They have Larry and Carol too but Larry and Carol are big and they don't want to play with us.

Miles and Sandy get a new house with a swimming pool in the basement. I wish we had a swimming pool in our basement. I love swimming so much Mommy says I'm a fish. I don't like the deep end of Miles' pool though because there's a whale in it. Daddy says there isn't, but I saw it. Daddy says, "It was just a shadow," but Daddy didn't see it. I did.

The water swishes around and our voices sound loud and we can all go swimming even if it's raining outside or cold or dark. Daddy says, "No, we can't have a pool in our basement, too." I hope it rains hard and it fills up with water anyway. We could jump off the steps.

Daddy shouts at me and I'm scared and I start to cry. We're having a Sunday school picnic at Mumma's Park and there's a Fellowship Meal in the pavilion. After that the children play children's games like Duck Duck Goose and Peanut Scramble and the daddies play volleyball and the mommies watch.

A thunderstorm comes up and it gets dark from the clouds and we have to all go in the pavilion because it's going to rain hard. It's going to rain *very* hard. It gets black like nighttime and very windy. The rain comes down so hard nobody can hear anybody talking and the mommies have to hold on to the picnic things or they'll blow away. All the air turns green and branches are breaking off the trees and my Daddy shouts at me. He shouts at me and yanks my hand so hard I drag through the air and over the ground while he runs to the car. He's yelling at me to hurry, but I'm falling down.

When we get into the car with Mommy and Kelly and the picnic things, Daddy says he's sorry he shouted at me. He was scared about the storm. He says when I was a baby he promised God he would never shout at his children unless something was very dangerous. Daddy keeps his promise. That's how I know the storm was very dangerous. Mommy and Daddy spank us sometimes when we're bad, but they never shout at us.

I hate potato soup. Mommy doesn't make it very much but when she does I have to eat it. I hate it. The potatoes are mushy and they're white like the warm milk they sit in and I hate it. I have to eat it anyway.

Everybody else gets done and goes into the living room and plays and watches TV and I'm sitting at the table because I hate potato soup. I won't get any dessert, either. I don't know why Mommy makes this when she knows I hate it. I like everything else in the world. Then Daddy comes back into the kitchen and says, "That's enough, Diana. You finish your soup right now, or I'll have to help you." That means he's going to spank me if I don't eat that horrible white goosh right now.

I start to cry because now the potato soup is cold and I hate it even more and Daddy doesn't care how much I hate it. When I get big I'm never going to eat potato soup and I won't make my children eat it either. I'm going to be nice to my children.

I wonder what a headache feels like. Mommy says, "I have a headache," and she has to go lie down. I don't think children get headaches, only grown-ups. I get bellyaches and leg aches and even earaches but they aren't the same as headaches.

Grandma Brubaker is at our house and I tell her I have a headache. I don't, but what if I did? I tell Grandma instead of Mommy because Mommy will know it isn't true. Or she might make me take a nap. Grandma looks worried and feels my head and asks if my belly feels alright. I say yes. Grandma asks Mommy for a Tylenol for me and Mommy asks, "What's the matter?" and Grandma tells her. Mommy looks at me funny, but she doesn't say anything so Grandma gives me the pill and I take it even though my head doesn't hurt.

Now, every time I hear about sins and lying, I think about how I told Grandma a lie. It was a lie. I said I had a headache, but I didn't. I don't know why I did that. The devil tricked me and made me sin. Now I have to ask Jesus to forgive me. I know that's not good enough, though. I have to ask *Grandma* to forgive me too or I could still go to hell if I die or if Jesus comes back. I'm embarrassed to tell Grandma I told her a lie. It takes me a really long time. I get a lot bigger. But I know I told a lie and I know I have to confess it to Grandma.

I finally do. By that time, I'm so big Grandma doesn't even remember, but she says she forgives me and she hugs me and says, "I'm really proud of you, Diana." I'm glad she ends up proud of me and now I can know my name is written in The Lamb's Book of Life. But I learned my lesson about lying: It doesn't seem like a very big deal until you have to tell on yourself so God can forgive you, and then it's really embarrassing.

I'm a lucky girl because I'm only five and already I know who I'm going to marry when I grow up. I'm going to marry Tommy Lehman. We're going to live in a stone house like his, not a wood house like mine, so that it can't catch on fire. Tommy goes to my church. He wants to be a fireman when he grows up. I want to be an acrobat.

Me and Tommy play "house" in Mommy's sewing room where we aren't supposed to play. I'm the mommy and he's the daddy. When it gets to be pretend nighttime, he says he has to lie right on me like mommies and daddies. I think that's a dumb idea. My daddy doesn't lie on my Mommy. Why would he do that? He's bigger than she is and she would get squashed. Besides, mommies and daddies always have big beds so there's room for both of them.

Mommy and Daddy would get really mad if they saw me and Tommy go into the bathroom together. I can go with girls like his little sister Missy, but not with boys. I make sure they don't see us. Tommy's lucky because he has a penis and he can go to the potty standing up. I have to pull my panties down and sit down. It must be nice to be a boy.

Kelly is so dumb she thinks that, because I'm going to marry Tommy, she can marry Missy. I tell her girls can't marry girls, but she doesn't care. I'm mad at her because she spied on me. Me and Tommy hid behind the couch in the living room so no one could see him give me a kiss on my cheek, but Kelly and Missy saw. I say, "He did not!" but he did and they know it.

Me and Tommy get bigger and go to school. There's a girl in Tommy's class named Susie Keller and he decides he's going to marry her instead. I don't think that's very nice of him to change his mind, but I guess it's alright. But the time I'm big enough to get married I might not like him very much anymore anyway. Besides, I could always marry Jeremy or Matthew or Eric.

Our town is Manheim. Manheim has Rettews and Weis Market and Rea & Derick Drugstore and Longenecker's Hardware and Twin Kiss.

I like Rettews. It's like an old house. The floor inside is wood and it thumps when you walk around. Upstairs are things for big people and downstairs are toys. We can only go down there if Mommy needs something from there because we always want something. They have coloring books and crayons and magic markers and hula hoops and jump ropes and tricycles and bicycles and Barbie dolls and baby dolls and little cars and big trucks and swimming pool toys and stuffed animals and plastic animals and whistles and yo-yos and lunch boxes and Etch-A-Sketches and Candy Land and Barrel-O-Monkeys and big balls and little balls and super balls and everything in the world. Upstairs in the back of Rettews are the shoes. Mommy buys us sneakers there and flip-flops for summer and boots for the rain and Sunday shoes for church. There's a fat old man who puts my foot inside a big metal foot to measure what size I wear. My shoes are the biggest because I'm the biggest. The cashier lady gives us lollipops like the bank lady.

Weis Market is a grocery store. I want to ride in the cart, but Kelly's littler than me so she rides in the cart and I have to walk. Mommy says I'm a big girl. I'm not a big girl. I'm a little girl. But Kelly's littler. When I was as little as Kelly we didn't have Kelly and I got to sit in the cart but it isn't fair because I don't remember it.

At the checkout, you put the food onto the counter and it rides all by itself up to the checkout lady. There's a blue stick you can put between your food and somebody else's if you don't want the lady in front of you to take your food. Mommy gives the checkout lady money and the checkout lady gives Mommy money and they both say, "Thank you."

Twin Kiss is for ice cream cones. Mommy never takes us there when we go shopping. Only Daddy takes us there sometimes on the way home from Grandma's house or programs at church. You can get chocolate, vanilla or mixed. I get mixed because that way you can have both. I lick real fast so it doesn't slop onto my dress.

Outside on the porch is the milk box. It's gray metal with a lid that opens and shuts. It has to stay shut so kitties don't get trapped in there. The Milk Man comes and puts full milks in the milk box. Mommy puts the empty ones in there at night and then she gets the full ones back out in the morning. I don't even know what The Milk Man looks like because he comes so early in the morning the sun isn't up and I'm not awake yet.

Who I do see is The Broom Man. The Broom Man sells brooms. If you don't know The Broom Man, you have to go to the store when you want a broom, but The Broom Man knows us, so he brings them to our house. The Broom Man's deaf and dumb.

It isn't nice to call people dumb, but this is a different kind of dumb that means you can't talk. I like The Broom Man because he's nice and he always gives me a yellow butterscotch sucking-candy. I feel sorry for him because he can't hear and he can't talk and everyone says he's dumb. It isn't that kind of dumb, but still, everyone says it and he can't even hear them. I wonder if he knows people say that. Anyway, it would be hard to be smart if you can't hear anything.

Mommy has a baby in her belly. She gets fat like a fat lady. We're going to the grocery store in the car and I'm in the back sitting on my side and Kelly is sitting on her side. I ask Mommy how she got that baby in there.

Mommy says something I can't believe. I think it's a trick, but Mommy isn't laughing and she never tries to trick us. She says God puts babies into mommies' bellies after the daddy puts his penis into her vagina. That's the middle hole in your bottom. She says mommies have eggs inside them and the daddies put sperms in there and then an egg starts growing into a baby in her belly.

I didn't know people had eggs. That doesn't sound very nice. I didn't know boys give off sperms, either. I wonder if there's any other way to get sperms in there. I can't believe Mommy and Daddy did that, but I guess if they want God to give them a baby, they have to. I guess that means everybody who has children has to get them that way. I thought God just put babies inside mommies when they pray and ask him for one.

I look out the window. We drive past the Faus' house and over the bridge in the meadow and come to the stop sign on Climer Road. I remember this. I'm thinking. I guess I won't have any babies when I'm big. I can't believe mommies and daddies have to do that—all mommies and daddies. This is a big surprise.

I wonder where mommies and daddies do this. It doesn't sound very easy. They must do it when no one else is looking because you have to pull down your underwear. I decide they must do it in the bathroom. It sounds pretty bathroomy to me. It sounds very yucky.

Mommy takes me to Manheim to get tested for kindergarten. I'm surprised you have to take a test before you even go to school. Mommy says they want to make sure all the children are ready. I know I am. Mommy takes me to a big school in Manheim, down some big halls to a big room where there are a lot of tables inside with activities. She has to wait in the hall and I have to go all by myself to the different tables. Some children are in the hall crying because they don't want to go in there without their mommies. I'm a little scared, but I want to go to kindergarten really bad so I go in.

It's an easy test. They make me say my name and pick things like the red triangle and the biggest ball and count how many and tie my shoe. I don't even have to write my name or say the ABC's. I don't have to say Bible verses or sing like in Sunday school. Then I have to walk backwards and hop on one foot and things like that. I didn't know you have to be able to do *that* to go to school. What about children in wheelchairs? But I guess there is a class called Jim and I don't guess they want children who fall down a lot. I tell the lady I can do flips.

I have a little white suitcase that used to be Mommy's when she was a girl. It's like a box with a lid and a handle and a clip that clicks it shut.

Grandma and Grandpa Brubaker come to our house to eat supper and play with us. I don't want them to go home. I tell Grandma I want to go home with her and sleep at her house. I know Mommy is going to say no, but she talks to Grandma and then she says, "Yes."

I run upstairs and get my white suitcase. I put my jammies in it and clean panties and a dress for tomorrow. I put on my coat and shoes and go home with Grandma and Grandpa.

Their car is green and it's lots bigger than ours. I sit in the backseat all by myself and I don't have to share with Kelly. Grandpa drives slow. It takes us a long time to get to Grandma's house but I don't care. I sit in the middle and smell the new-car smell of Grandma and Grandpa's big green car. I have my white suitcase with my jammies beside me. I pretend I'm going far far away; just me with Grandma and Grandpa.

There's a big bush outside the house and a mommy duck from down at the pond comes up here and makes her nest under it. She lays eggs in it and she sits on them. She's brown and she has a flat funny beak that she sticks out at me when I come look at her. She doesn't like me. Maybe she thinks I'm going to shoot her like in Duck Season or take away her eggs and eat them. I'm not. I want to pet her, but she doesn't like me and acts like she wants to peck me.

Mommy and Daddy say, "Leave that duck alone." If I go too close, she could peck me really hard. Also, if she gets scared, she might go away and never come back and her duckies would have to stay inside those eggs and never come out.

Sometimes I look under the bush and the mother duck isn't there. I crawl under and look at the eggs. There are a lot of them, piled up on top of each other. They look just like chicken eggs only a little bigger. Mommy finds me and says, "Diana Renee, I told you to leave that duck alone." I tell her the duck isn't there, only the eggs. She says I have to leave the nest alone too or the mother duck will be able to tell I was touching them and she'll go away and not come back.

Leaving it alone is very hard.

After a while, the mother duck stops sitting on her nest because she has baby duckies but there's still eggs in there. She forgot about some of them. She must not be a very good mother after all if she forgets about some of her own eggs. Mommy says, "Leave those eggs alone—they're rotten." Mommy says if they didn't hatch into duckies, they were no good in the first place.

I don't think I believe her. How would my Mommy know that? I think there's still baby duckies inside those eggs, but they can't come out because their mommy won't sit on them and keep them warm. I wish I could get them out. I wish I could sit on them, but I'm too big and I would smash them.

Then I have a very good idea. Baby duckies can swim as soon as they're born so I could put the leftover eggs into warm water—not too hot—and then the baby duckies could come out. That would be nice of me. I'm pretty smart. Then the duckies would think I'm their mommy and they would like me. I could pet them and feed them and teach them to swim.

I put the leftover eggs into my dress and I go into the bathroom when Mommy's not looking. Mommy would tell me, "No." I fill up the sink with warm water and I put the eggs in it. I stir them around a little, very carefully. I'm very quiet so Mommy won't say, "What are you doing in there?" I hope they hatch quick.

Then something terrible happens. All of the sudden the eggs burst open and horrible brown goo comes shooting out all over me and all over the bathroom and it stinks worse than anything and there aren't any duckies. I'm scared and upset and I start to scream and cry when the eggs explode. Mommy is knocking on the bathroom door saying, "What's the matter, Diana? Open the door!"

I cry and cry and I can't stop. She's going to smack me for sure about this mess and about disobeying. I tell her about the duckies.

I have to take a bath and change my dress, but she doesn't smack me because I'm already crying. She just says, "That's why I told you to leave them alone—because they're rotten."

I didn't know what a rotten egg meant before but now I do.

We have a fox. He's a red fox. He lives in a fox pen Daddy made behind the barn. Daddy feeds him dead chickens and gives him water. Daddy likes him a lot. He says he's pretty. He is pretty and he has a pretty tail. We can look at him, but we can't touch him. If we stick our finger in there, he'll bite us. I poke a stick in his cage and he says "Kgha! Kgha!" and bites the stick.

I ask Daddy if we should let him out. Daddy says we can't let him out. He says he found that fox and some other baby foxes in the field without a mommy when he was plowing. He says if we let him out, he'll die because he doesn't know how to be a real fox and catch things to eat.

Poor fox. I think he wants to go out, but he has to stay in.

Mrs. Kilmer lives on Kilmer Road. Sometimes she keeps us when Mommy has to go away. Mrs. Kilmer's boys and girls are big and they don't live at her house anymore but Mrs. Kilmer is a smart lady because she saved all their toys from when they were little. She has them in a closet. Mrs. Kilmer has a big plastic airplane that opens up and toy people can sit inside. It doesn't fly, though—it only drives.

Mrs. Kilmer is a Brethren. That means she can get her hair cut, but she still loves God and goes to church. Mommy goes to the ladies' Bible Study at Mrs. Kilmer's house and then there are lots of children and we have to share the toys. I like it better when just me and Kelly go there.

I think it might be nicer to be a Brethren like Mrs. Kilmer because then we could get our hair cut if we wanted but we would still go to heaven. I guess Grandma wouldn't like it if we started being Brethrens, though.

We go to the shore with Miles and Sandy. It's called Assateague and we put up a big green tent in the campground that we all can sleep in. We can play in the sand all day, and in the water, but we have to be careful because the ocean is dangerous. It has waves that can get you. It tastes yucky like salt too. And there are green flies that bite you. And sand gets into your eyes. Mommy doesn't want us to get sand in the tent, but the sand is on us and it just comes in. And it rains so our things get wet. And we scream because the flies bite us and it hurts.

After that Mommy and Daddy don't want to go to the shore anymore. They say, "That's why we like going to the mountains." I like going to the mountains too, but I think the shore might be all right if you went to a different one besides Assateague.

E rnie is my biggest cousin. He's Uncle Eugene's boy and he goes to Grandma Zimmerman's house. At Grandma Brubaker's house, I'm the biggest. Before we go home Grandma Zimmerman gives us white ice cream with chocolate syrup. I like chocolate but not chocolate syrup, so I just eat my ice cream plain. Ernie says, "Put chocolate syrup on, it tastes good." I tell him I don't like it. He says, "Did you ever try it?" I say, "no." He tells me to try it. I don't like it, but I decide to guess I could try.

It's really good. You can mix it around and make regular chocolate ice cream out of it right in your dish. Then you never have to eat plain ice cream anymore. I like Ernie.

We're going to church in the car and Daddy has to hurry up to lead the singing. Mommy says, "Lamar, you better watch it. You don't want to get stopped." If you drive too fast a police can catch you and get you in trouble. Big people can't usually get in trouble, but a policeman can give you a ticket or make you go to jail.

We go around the corner and there is a policeman in his car and he starts driving after us with his lights flashing like Daddy did something bad. Daddy says, "Oh boy," and Mommy says, "That rascal," because he was waiting for people going to church in a hurry. He must be an extra bad police.

I'm scared. In storybooks, police are nice and help children find the way home when they get lost in cities. But we aren't in a city and we aren't lost and real police have guns and they could shoot you if they think you're really bad.

Daddy has to stop driving beside the road. Mommy says, "It's okay, girls," but me and Kelly are very very scared. We get down on the floor of our sides and try to hide from him. I don't want the policeman to see me. I don't know what policemen do to little girls if their daddies do something bad. I'm afraid he's going to do something to Daddy or make him go to jail like a bad person.

The policeman comes over to the window and I hear him talk to Daddy. He isn't very nice. The policeman says Daddy was going too fast and Daddy says he's sorry. The policeman doesn't care. He can see Mommy and Daddy are going to church and he doesn't care. I hope he can't see me down here on the floor. If he sees me hiding, he might think I did something bad too and he might get me. It's cold outside and cold air is coming into the car.

Then the policeman goes away and we can close the window and drive to church. That police didn't do anything to Daddy and I don't think he saw me and Kelly because he didn't try to get us.

Now we're *really* late and we can't even hurry.

I heard of children who say bad words getting their mouths washed out with soap. I never say bad words because Jesus can always hear me and bad words make Jesus sad. I think about getting your mouth washed out with soap. It probably doesn't taste very good. But it must be a good idea—you wash everything else with soap, and your hair you wash with shampoo. I decide it might be a good thing to wash my mouth with soap because I'm never going to say bad words and my mouth probably needs to be washed.

There's green Lava soap in the bathroom for when Daddy comes in from the barn and I wash my mouth with it. It tastes very very yucky. It's a pretty good punishment for bad children.

I ask Mommy if it's a good idea to wash your mouth with soap because then I'm going to tell her I already did it all by myself.

Mommy says, "Oh no, Honey. That's why we brush our teeth every day."

I say, "Oh."

I guess that means toothpaste is soap too and it isn't even yucky like Lava. I guess I did that for nothing.

Sometimes we go to church at South Christian Street. It takes a long time to get there because it's in the city where the buildings reach up to the sky and you have to be quiet or everyone will look at you. I like South Christian Street. Mommy and Daddy used to go there before I was born when they lived in the trailer and Daddy was a carpenter. Jim Weaver is the preacher and he has a shiny head and black people go to church there. I like seeing black people because we don't have any at our regular church and neither does Grandma Brubaker or Grandma Zimmerman. It's because our churches aren't in the city and black people live in the city.

South Christian Street has white people too. Jodi and Marcy are in my Sunday school class and they're white like me. Nancy is our teacher. Nancy is always sad because she isn't very pretty and her face is red. Audreen is in Kelly's class. She's little and skinny and kind of brownish and she's always scared and never says anything. I like her because she has about a million pigtails. I only have two.

Jim Weaver, the preacher, is Marcy's daddy. He looks like a giant when he preaches up there and all the people listen because he talks really loud and walks around and almost starts crying sometimes. Marcy's mommy's name is Roseen. She's lucky her mommy and daddy have names like Jim and Roseen. My mommy and daddy are Ruth and Lamar. Jim and Roseen sound like names on TV.

In the city, there are bad people who don't go to church. I see them walking on the street when we get out of the car and go inside or when we are ready to go home. One of them lives beside the parking lot and she sits up on her balcony in her housecoat and looks at us but she doesn't get dressed and come down. These people must be the ones who aren't Christians and are going to hell. I'm scared of them. I look at them to see what people who don't have Jesus in their hearts look like. I hope some of them go to a different church that's already over or maybe didn't start yet because I don't want all of them to go to hell. When I grow up I'm going to live in a big city and be a missionary who tells people about Jesus and that they better go to church.

Mommy has two piles of dresses in her room, one for me and one for Kelly. They're ready so we can take them to Grandma's house when Mommy has her baby. She's going to have it soon and I'm glad because I love going to Grandma's house. I put things in my little white suitcase.

I hope Mommy has a boy. I already have Kelly and one little sister is enough—it better not be another girl. When the baby is ready to come out Mommy can feel it and she has to go to the hospital and it will come out there.

Daddy goes away and comes home with a color TV. It's the biggest TV in the world and now Mr. Greenjeans' jeans are really green. The other TV was little and sat on a stool and all the colors were gray. It didn't work so good anymore so Daddy went to the store and bought a new one. It's bigger than me. It's so big it doesn't need a stool—it just sits on the floor in its own wood box.

Mommy doesn't like it. She thinks it's too big and too pretty. Mommy doesn't like TV very much, but Daddy says he always wanted a color TV. Mommy thinks Grandma won't like it.

I don't know why Grandma would care about the TV because when Grandma and Grandpa come, we have to turn it off anyway.

It's almost Christmas and my favorite book is called *'Twas the Night Before Christmas*. Every day before nap and before bed, Mommy says, "Okay, girls. You can each pick a book," and I pick *'Twas the Night Before Christmas* a lot. It's a poem and it rhymes.

Mommy reads it so much that I learn it and I can read it too. I'm a smart girl. I didn't even go to kindergarten yet and I can read a book. Mommy tells me to read it to Grandma. Grandma has a funny smile on her face and she says, "Isn't that something? It looks just like she's reading! And she even turns the page at the right place." She shakes her head and says "Tst-tst-tst" with her teeth. "Isn't that something, Grandpa?"

Grandpa thinks it's "Something," too.

But I don't understand why they say it looks like I'm reading. I *am* reading! I look at the pages and say what the words are and then I turn it and say the next ones. That's what Mommy does when she reads. That's what all big people do when they read. I can even read it in my head to myself like Daddy does when he studies the Sunday school lesson. I'm really Something.

I have a Christmas present for Daddy. He's going to like it a lot; I know because it's a book he reads every day for Sunday school. He's looking for it all over the place and so is Mommy, but they can't find it because I'm hiding it up in my room. I'm happy because that was a smart idea—imagine how glad Daddy is going to be when he sees I gave him his favorite book. It isn't really that close to Christmas yet so he'll probably forget and be really surprised. Mommy does that with our toys sometimes. Not for Christmas, though.

On Christmas, Daddy is *very* surprised. Even Mommy is surprised and they laugh their heads off. They can't believe I thought of that idea all by myself. Daddy says I shouldn't take people's things and hide them because people need their things. He sure is happy to have that book, though, just like I thought.

Kelly doesn't just get up when she wakes up, she calls for Mommy and Mommy has to come upstairs or Kelly will cry. Kelly calls for Mommy and Mommy doesn't answer. Kelly calls more and then the stairway door opens and it isn't Mommy down there. It's Grandma Zimmerman. She comes upstairs and says, "Girls, your Mommy isn't here. She went to the hospital to have her baby."

Kelly cries because Mommy isn't here, but I'm excited because Grandma is. Well, actually I'm sad because it's better to take your dresses in a suitcase and go stay at Grandma's house but the baby wanted to come out in the night when we were sleeping. Too bad. Daddy's in the hospital with Mommy too. I ask Grandma if it's a girl or a boy and Grandma doesn't know yet.

We go downstairs and eat Cheerios and then Daddy calls on the telephone and tells Grandma it's not a boy. It's a girl. Another one.

I'm mad. I don't want another dumb old girl. We have enough girls. I can't believe God didn't give us a boy. Can't he see we already have girls? Now I have to have *two* sisters for the rest of my whole life. Grandma says her name is Michelle Cherie. I don't really care what her name is. I wanted a boy.

Mommy looks little when she brings her baby home from the hospital. She looks very skinny and she always says she's tired. I don't know why since at the hospital you just lie in bed and the nurses take care of you. And babies don't even do anything except sleep—at least ours doesn't.

The baby sucks milk out of Mommy and I think it's kind of yucky. It seems like something for puppies and kitties and cows.

"Baby Michelle has such a head of black hair!" That's what everybody says. She wakes up and cries and she drinks milk and sleeps and Mommy has to change her diaper. That's about all. We can't even hold her by ourselves because her head flops around too much. Mommy says we can when she's bigger, but I want to hold her now. When she's bigger, it won't be as fun. I like to watch Mommy give her a bath. There's a brown thing in her belly button that you can't touch and it's going to fall off by itself. It's yucky. I like her all right but I thought you could play with babies more. And I really wanted a boy.

Now that we have baby Michelle lots of company comes over and I love company. Everybody brings baby presents, though, and hardly anybody remembers about me and Kelly. Me and Kelly like presents and that baby doesn't even know about presents. We have to open them for her. Some people think about us too and bring us candy or coloring books or something. There should be a rule about that. Everybody has to hold Baby Michelle and say how cute she is and how much hair. I have way more hair than that. Kelly too. People tell us we're big. Well, we're bigger than the baby, but we're not that big. We still like presents.

Sometimes at bedtime Mommy is busy with Baby Michelle and she can't tuck us in. Then Daddy does it and I love it when Daddy tucks me in. He tries to do it like Mommy, but it's different. I get under my covers and Daddy sits on the side of my bed so we can say our prayers. I say "Now I Lay Me Down To Sleep" and then I make up a little prayer like dear Jesus thank you for this nice day and thank you for the snow in Jesus' name amen. Then Daddy says a bigger prayer for me and everything else and says "In Jesus' Name Amen."

Then, if Daddy isn't in a hurry, he keeps sitting there and I ask him what things are made of. I ask him what material is made of and he says it comes from plants that grow called cotton. And some other kinds grow on sheep. I ask him what metal is made of and he says it comes out of the ground and gets melted into things we can use. I ask him what paper is made of and he tells me it comes from trees. That's hard to imagine. Paper is soft and trees are hard. My favorite one is glass because Daddy says glass is made of sand. I don't see how they do that because you can see through glass, but you can't see through sand and sand is nice but glass can cut you. Daddy says they have to kind of cook it. Then I wonder who thought up cooking sand.

One day when we go to Twin Kiss I think about ice cream cones and I ask Daddy what ice cream cones are made of. He says he doesn't know, but he thinks maybe sawdust. I think after that Mommy probably won't let us have them anymore, but she does. I guess a little bit isn't too bad for you.

Mommy hangs Bible verses on the 'frigerator and we have to say them before we pray so we can eat. I don't really like that, but I can't say it because God wouldn't like it if he knew I don't like Bible verses.

Because I *do* like Bible verses. I can say "For God so loved the world" and "The Lord is my shepherd" and "Do unto others." I just don't like to have to say them with Kelly when it's dinnertime. I'm hungry and now we have to say verses *and* pray. And Mommy always picks dumb ones about being good like "Children obey your parents" and "A soft answer turneth away wrath" and "Thy Word have I hid in my heart that I might not sin against Thee."

I always try to learn them faster than Kelly because I'm bigger and I have to be smarter. Also, I don't want Jesus to be sad and think I don't love the Bible. Because I do.

I like to play drums. I don't have a real drum because they're too noisy, but when Mommy plays the piano and Daddy plays the guitar, I can play on a kettle. Mommy has some great big kettles and wooden spoons are just like drumsticks if you use the other end.

Mommy and Daddy are singing and playing and I want to play too. Mommy says I'm big enough to go get my own kettle to drum on so I go out to the kitchen and turn the light on. The cabinet where the big kettles are is tall and white and metal. One door never opens right and the biggest kettle is on that side. Mommy puts them on the bottom so I can get them, but the big one's in the back. I hold on to the handle of the stuck door and yank it with all my might. I'm a very strong little girl and I can do it myself.

The door yanks open and the whole cabinet rocks. Then Mommy's big glass pitcher that is special and only for company falls off the top shelf and hits me right on the head. The pouring thing hits me right on the forehead underneath my bangs.

I scream and cry and blood starts running out my head. Then I scream and cry more. It really hurts and I know about what happens to people when they break their heads. They die.

There's blood coming out my head and I'm crying and crying because I'm only five and I don't want to die and go to heaven. I want to go to kindergarten. I wanted to die when I'm an old lady like Grandma, not now when I'm five and I just wanted to drum on a kettle.

Daddy holds me on the rocking chair and Mommy puts a cloth on my head and calls the doctor. I keep waiting to see Jesus or angels or something, but the only thing that happens is that my head really hurts.

I ask Daddy, "How long is it until I die?"

Daddy laughs a little and says, "Oh, Honey. You're not going to die. You just have a cut and you're going to be okay. We're going to go to the doctor so he can sew it shut and you can go to school next week."

Oh. I stop crying because I'm not going to die after all. I do get to go to kindergarten! I thought if your head bleeds, you die.

Mommy and Daddy drive to the doctor in the dark. I've been to the doctor's lots of times but not in the dark. They take me back into the emergency side where I never went either. Doctor Godshall is my doctor, but he isn't there because it's nighttime and he's at home eating supper. Some other doctor gets me and he makes me lie down and he sticks a needle into my sore head and sews it like a torn dress. I scream because it hurts worse than the pitcher and Mommy and Daddy have to hold on to me so I don't get up.

He wraps a bandage all the way around and around my head like an Indian and I can't take it off. Now I'm happy again. It's pretty special to have your head bandaged up. Everyone can see I almost died. Kelly doesn't get to have a bandage, only me. Now I do look like an Indian, especially because I have pigtails. Maybe when I go to kindergarten Mommy will let me stick feathers into it.

PART TWO

CHICKEN TEETH

I get school shoes for kindergarten and a red book bag and some socks and a new dress. My school is called Mastersonville Elementary and Mommy has to take me there in the car because there isn't any kindergarten in the morning when the bus gets the big kids. When you're in kindergarten, you have to wait until after dinner to go to school because some children cry if they have to stay away from their mommies that long. Not me.

Regular school isn't like Sunday school. There's lots more kids and the teacher doesn't have a helper. We have to sit in the same chair every day. There's six chairs at my table and we all have to share crayons. We get the big fat kind because we're little, and if we get little ones we might break them. I have little crayons at home but I kind of like the fat ones in kindergarten. Sometimes we have to wait until our neighbor is done with the yellow or red and we can't grab or be mean.

Our room has lots of windows and a blackboard and tables and chairs and a playhouse and a jungle gym and Miss Jennings. Miss Jennings is the prettiest teacher in the whole school. We have cubbyholes with our names on them for our coats and book bags.

We have "Milk Break" in the afternoon when we get to pick chocolate or white. We have to raise our hand for which one we want. I pick chocolate.

In the front of our room above the blackboard are the ABC's that I already know and the numbers that I know too and a clock and the flag. Miss Jennings teaches us to say "I Pledgeallegiance." I like I Pledgeallegiance because it has big words like on the news and the president.

Daddy doesn't know if it's ok to say I Pledgeallegiance because we have to love God more than the flag. Mommy says it's all right because we're thankful to God that we live in America and anyway it says "under God." After "under God" it says "invisible." I guess because God is invisible because America sure isn't and the flag isn't either. Anyway, no one could love the flag more than God. Except maybe if they don't go to church.

Mary Jane's last name is Zimmerman too and she sits beside me at my table. Amy Wilson sits on the other side of me. Her one eye is shut so she can only look out of the other one. Mary Jane has pigtails like me because she's a Mennonite too and so is Cindy Myers and Billy Brubaker, but he doesn't count because he's a boy and boys don't have to wear anything special in the Bible. Girls have to wear dresses and we have to have long hair to show we love God.

I don't really like to play with Cindy and Mary Jane. They're quiet and shy and Mary Jane is scared. She cries when Miss Jennings calls on her. Mommy says Mary Jane doesn't understand Miss Jennings because they talk Pennsylvania Dutch at her house. Mary Jane probably isn't dumb, but she can't spell Mary Jane when it's her turn, so she gets sent out of kindergarten to a school for children who aren't smart enough. Now no one sits on my other side.

Amy is lucky because when it's her turn to spell her name and get a marshmallow she always gets it right: A-M-Y. I get mine right too because D-I-A-N-A is easy, but I feel sorry for Matthew because he has to say M-A-T-T-H-E-W.

Poor Mary Jane. It isn't fair for the dumbest girl to have the longest name.

Karen Groff is in my class too and she's our neighbor. Her mommy's name is Evelyn and her daddy's name is Bob and they have a baby like Michelle but they got a boy. His name is Bobby. Karen is littler than me, but she's five too. I like Karen.

We have rest time at school. I love rest time. Miss Jennings gives us mats and we have to lie on the floor and act like we're sleeping. Sometimes the bad boys like Mike Travis make snoring noises and we all think it's funny except Miss Jennings. She doesn't get to have rest time, she has to sit at her desk and watch us or we'll be bad.

I hate nap time at home, but I like rest time at school. I lie on my mat and look sideways across the blue floor at all the legs of the tables and chairs. I see all the other girls and boys lying on their mats and you can hear Miss Jennings at her desk turning the pages.

Now I get to go to a new Sunday school class too. I don't have to go in the little kids' class anymore with Kelly, I go to the kindergarten class with Tommy and Johnny and Darvin and Sharon. We each get a Bible all of our very own. It comes in a box with Jesus and the disciples and Noah and Moses and Mary and Abraham and everybody on it. The Bible inside it has that too and it's pretty and perfect and new and it's the Holy Word of God.

Now I'm big and I can read the Bible and be a Christian too. Only I can't read yet. But I write D-I-A-N-A in it in case it gets lost and so it won't get confused with anybody else's. This one is mine. The pages are thin like tissue paper and in the back when you get to Jesus, everything he said is red. That way it isn't hard to tell what the most important rules are. The whole Bible's important, but Jesus is the best part. I hold my Bible and open it and look in it at the words and the pictures. Now I *know* God can see me because I have his Word in my hands and he can see me looking at it.

Mommy likes Baby Michelle's hair because it's black and curly. Mommy said when I was a baby I didn't have any hair, I just had peach fuzz. If I had on pants in the winter people thought I was a boy.

Mommy combs Baby Michelle's hair dumb. She combs it all straight up to the top and makes it into a curl and Daddy says she looks so pretty. I don't think she looks pretty like that. Who ever heard of combing all your hair up to one big curl on the top? I think it looks stupid. I don't say so, though. Everybody else says she looks so cute just like an Indian baby with all that black hair.

I'm six and I get a barn for my birthday. It's called an Activity Barn and inside are a million things for making things. It has coloring books and crayons and scissors and paper and glue and stencils and tape . . . It's like a big box full of everything only it's shaped like a barn with a handle on top. It's my favorite thing I ever got in my whole life. I can color and paste and draw and cut and trace and paint. I love it.

When you go to school, you get to go on field trips but it doesn't mean you go to a field. Miss Jennings takes us on a Field Trip to Yellow Freight where all the big trucks are. I thought that on Field Trips, you got to go to exciting places you didn't know about and Yellow Freight is on the way to Grandma's. But I never went in it before.

For field trips, your class gets on the bus after you get to school. It's funny to get on the bus with the teacher! "Room mothers" come on field trips, too. Room mothers are other people's mommies that come along to help Miss Jennings make us be good. Maybe my mommy could be a Room mother sometime. Everyone will have to be *very* good.

We get to see inside one of the big trucks at Yellow Freight and we have to sit down and a man tells us about how big and important Yellow Freight is. He tells us why the Yellow Freight trucks are all orange. It's because the man who made Yellow Freight was color-blind and he didn't know what it was. Color-blind means you can still see things, but they all look black and white like on our old TV.

I count to one hundred all by myself. We go to visit Grandma and Grandpa Brubaker and everyone is watching Baby Michelle. I'm sitting on Grandpa's lap and I wonder how you count to a hundred. That's a lot of numbers. I count to ten in my head. Then I know eleven, twelve up to twenty. Then thirty-one, thirty-two. Then comes forties. Then fifties. I count the sixties and the seventies and eighties. Then comes nine so I count all the nineties, but I get stuck when it ends at ninety-nine. I wonder if one hundred is next and I think it might be.

I say, "Grandpa," but Grandpa is talking.

I say, "Grandpa" again but Grandpa is still talking and if I pester him, Mommy will tell me about it later.

I have to wait until he gets done and says, "What?" to ask him what comes after ninety-nine.

Grandpa says, "A hundred."

I can't believe it. I did it! I counted to a hundred all by myself right here in Grandpa's lap and it wasn't even hard!

Robbie and Billy Brubaker and Chris get into an argument about which one is going to marry me when we get big. I sit on the top of the jungle gym and look at them. I don't know which one is the best. Not Chris, but I like Robbie *and* Billy. Probably Billy because Billy is a Brubaker like Grandma Brubaker and besides Robbie is littler than Kelly.

Me and Kelly have a lot of things we play. Sometimes we play "Girl," where one is the mother and the other one is the girl. Also, there's "Sick Girl," where the girl is sick and the mother has to take care of her.

We make up games too. One game is "Slap," where we stand apart and swing our hands and sometimes they smack into each other. It's funny and it kind of hurts. We also made up "Trap." For Trap, one girl has to lie on the floor with her legs apart and wait. The other girl walks all around and pretends like she doesn't see the trap and, when she steps in it, the legs go shut and she gets caught. She screams and pretends like she's very surprised. That game's really funny.

The best game we have is called "Sorry Sir." Sorry Sir is like a play because we both have to pretend to be someone like an old man or a funny lady or a blind person. We walk along and bang right into each other. Then we act surprised and say, "Sorry, sir," in pretend voices. Every time we turn around and do it again, we pretend to be someone different until we can't think up any more people to be.

Sometimes Mommy lets me and Kelly play with Baby Michelle. We can put her in the dolly crib and put the dolly blankets on her. She doesn't like it much, though, and starts to cry. She's just a baby so she doesn't know we're trying to be nice and play with her. She likes the coach, though. We have an old coach for our dollies that's a real baby coach, but old. We can push her in the coach and she likes that. We have to be very careful and Mommy watches us to make sure we are.

I get to go to Student Council. One boy or girl from each grade goes to a special meeting with the principal, but not because we were bad. It's just so we can all talk about school. Mr. Fallinger is a nice man, but I'm afraid of him because he's the principal and he's allowed to spank you. The big boys and girls talk to Mr. Fallinger about things like recess and lunchtime and field trips and I'm allowed to say whatever I want, but I don't want to say anything. Not around Mr. Fallinger!

Some days we have Story Time and Miss Jennings sits on the floor with us and reads us stories. I love Story Time. We get to sit wherever we want to, but we have to be quiet or Story Time is over and you can't hear the end.

I have a comb and I'm combing my hair and being quiet. I decide to make curls. I take some hair and wrap it around and around and around the comb, like ladies on TV do with curlers. When I think my curls are ready I unwind my comb. It doesn't unwind right so I wrap it back up again and try it again. Then it really doesn't unwind right and I can't get it out. I know I'm going to get in trouble with Miss Jennings *and* Mommy if I can't get it out, but I'm doing my best and it won't come out. I tear some of my hairs, but that hurts. I can see this wasn't such a good idea after all.

After the story, Miss Jennings sees what I did. She can't get it out either and she isn't very happy with me. She has to cut it out with a scissors and she takes my comb away.

All the girls in my class like Matthew. I would like Matthew too, but it isn't fair for all the girls to like one boy so I like Matthew's friend Jeremy Johnson. Jeremy has a brother in the army, which might mean they don't love God in their family because soldiers kill people. But Jeremy isn't in the army, he's only in kindergarten with me. I think it's ok for me to like him. I'm only little.

I want to give Jeremy a present—a real present—but I don't know what. When I want to give Grandma a present or Mommy, I color them a picture or something like that. But I can't color Jeremy a picture. I try to think of what to make him, but I can't think of anything he would like. I can't buy him a present because I'm too little for money and, besides, I can't go to the store by myself. I think about this and then I remember something. Up on the shelf in the sewing room is a cup where Mommy put money that people gave Baby Michelle for baby presents. What a dumb thing to give a baby! Mommy and Daddy already have money; why in the world does Baby Michelle need it? If I'm too little for money, she's *way* too little.

I climb up there and get it down because I think people like money and maybe that would be a nice present for Jeremy. There's all different numbers on the money and I pick a five because one doesn't seem like very much but ten and twenty are big numbers. Five is about right. I give Jeremy five dollars and he likes it just like I thought. I think that might have been naughty because I don't think Mommy would like me giving presents to boys, but I want to. I'm just being nice like I'm supposed to be.

Miss Jennings gives me a note for Mommy and I give it to her like Miss Jennings says. Then Mommy calls me and I see the five dollars I gave Jeremy is in the note from Miss Jennings. I can see I was way worse than I thought I was.

Mommy asks me what I did and I tell her I gave Jeremy a present. She asks me where I got it and I tell her. She says Jeremy's mommy sent the money back. She says children have no business with money, that if I want to give Jeremy a present, I should *make* him something. Mommy tells me that taking things—even extra money in your own house—that don't belong to you is stealing. Then I know that I was *very* bad by accident. I didn't think it was stealing if the other person didn't need it. I feel sorry and ashamed because I would never steal things, but I accidentally did. Now I'm embarrassed and I don't want to see Mommy or Daddy or Miss Jennings or Jeremy. Mommy tells me not to take any more money out of the cup, but I already wouldn't. She didn't have to tell me that. Especially since she put it away someplace I never saw again.

Kelly gets stung by a bee because her shirt has flowers on it and bees like it. I have one like that too only mine's bigger, but after that bee stings Kelly I don't wear my flower shirt to play outside anymore. Mommy says it's alright, it's not because of the flowers— sometimes bees just sting people. I know they do, but they sting you more if you wear a shirt with big bright flowers. Kelly doesn't wear her flower shirt anymore, either. Mommy might as well give them to Aunt Judy for Kristen and Katrina.

We have a special surprise at school for Christmas. All the tables and chairs are pushed away to the back and we aren't going to learn anything today, we're going to watch a movie. Movies are the best, even better than filmstrips, and the whole school is coming down to the kindergarten room to watch. All the teachers are coming too. Even the principal, Mr. Fallinger. We all sit on the floor and Mr. Fallinger turns the lights off and we can't start until we all be quiet. Some of the big boys are bad.

When the projector comes on we all say "Five! Four! Three! Two! One!" when the numbers come on and then there's some music and Jiminy Cricket. There's Geppetto and Pinocchio just like in the book Mommy reads us at home, but in the movie they talk. Everybody in the whole school laughs.

When it's over, the screen goes bright and the end of the tape makes a smacking noise and nobody wants to go home.

We have four chicken houses for the chickens to live in. Before the baby chicks come, big trucks bring shavings that are made of wood and smell good. They put them all over the floor for the peepies to walk in. Then the chicken trucks come from Longeneckers Hatchery with boxes of peepies. The men stack the boxes inside the doors of the chicken houses and Daddy and the men dump them out onto the floor under the brooders where it's hot. When I get big enough, I can help too. Daddy dumps the ones on top and I dump the ones on the bottom that I can reach. You have to be very very careful when you dump chicks! You have to be careful not to step on them because they're just born and they don't know you're not their mommy and they follow you. Also, you have to be careful not to throw them out too hard or you can hurt them. But you have to throw them a little bit hard because if they land back in the box you have to throw them again and it's not good for them. And you have to be really quiet or you'll scare them. I'm good at it and I like helping Daddy. I hardly ever smash any of them.

The chicks get bigger and bigger and they start to grow feathers and look really ugly. Daddy has to walk through all the chicken houses every day and pick up the dead ones because some always die. We have to count the dead ones so Weavers can see if Daddy is doing a good job. The dead ones that aren't rotten we give to the kitties and doggies. If we find a sick one or one that can't walk, we have to kill it because it's going to die. Daddy says the other chickens will peck it to death so it doesn't eat their food. Daddy shows me how to break their necks on the bucket. I can do it if they're little, but when they get big Daddy has to do it because I only choke them.

When the chickens get big I can't go into the chicken house without a special mask like Daddy because me and Daddy get asthma.

Then at the end, when the chickens are big enough, the "chicken catchers" come and get them. They come when it's dark so that they can open all the doors and the chickens won't run away. They catch all the chickens and put them into crates on a big truck and they go away to get killed. Sometimes Mommy or Daddy goes to Dunkin Donuts and buys donuts for the chicken catchers to give them a surprise. The chicken catchers come in a van and we never see them because we aren't allowed to go outside while they're here. We don't know those men and we don't know if they're good or bad so we can't go near them.

Sometimes the chicken catchers forget some chickens and we find them later. Then Daddy catches them and chops their heads off on the chopping block in the barn. Daddy says they are dead right away, but they don't look like it! After their head is off, they jump up and run all around and fall because they can't see and they get blood all over the place and kick and flap all over the barn. I don't like that part. It would be funny if its head wasn't off.

Then Mommy dunks them in a dishpan of hot, hot water and pulls out their feathers. I don't like pulling out the feathers that much because they stick to my fingers, but I like the next part. Daddy cuts them open and I can pull out their insides. It's warm and squishy and a little yucky, but their intestines are different colors and Daddy shows me the gizzards where there is still chicken feed and the hearts that are soft and red and sometimes in girl chickens we find little yellow eggs.

When summer comes kindergarten is over and I have to stay home all day. Mommy takes me and Karen to Manheim Pool for swimming lessons. Mommy doesn't know how to swim because Grandma never let her go in the water so now if she falls in, she could drown. She doesn't want us to drown, so she takes us to swimming lessons. I love swimming lessons because I love swimming.

Our teacher is a big fat lady and since we're the littlest ones we have to sit in the baby pool where it isn't even deep. I don't see how you can learn to swim in the baby pool. She tells us we can't learn to swim right away because first we have to learn to do the "dead man's float" and she shows us how. She lies flat down in the water and floats on her face. That's easy. Some of the boys and girls are crying because they're scared and they don't want to put their faces into the water but not me. I can put my face into the water.

When it's my turn, the fat lady holds me under until I almost drown. She's a very mean lady. She makes me lie down and I do and she makes me put my face into the water, but when I try to lift it up again, she keeps holding me down under the water and I can't come up. That's a terrible thing to do to children! She holds me down on the bottom of the baby pool and I know she doesn't care if I die.

She lets me come up before I drown. At first I'm very mad at her for that, but then I can see that she does this so we won't be afraid to go underwater anymore. I guess she's kind of right—I didn't know someone could hold you under water and you wouldn't die. But some children cry too much and if you don't take a turn getting held underwater by the fat lady, you can't take swimming lessons and your mommy has to take you home and you can't learn how to swim.

122

I like going fishing with Daddy. Me and Daddy get the bucket and the shovel from the barn and we go dig up some worms. We always find lots of worms in the dirt down by the loading chute at the barn. Some little girls are scared of worms but not me. Not even big ones.

Then Daddy gets the fishing poles and we go down to the pond. I have to be quiet or all the fish get scared and swim away. Daddy puts the worm on the hook for me so I don't poke myself. I feel sorry for the little worms getting a hook stuck into them, but Daddy says they don't have any feelings. I think they do have feelings because when you poke him, he wiggles a lot. But I guess it doesn't matter because anyway he's going to drown in the water and get ate by a fish. You have to poke the worm's tail and push him up along the hook until the hook is all full of worm, and if you don't do it right, a smart fish could bite him off the hook and not get caught. And if the worm is too big to fit the whole thing on, you can just tear it in half. It's alright to do that because it can grow the other half back. I can see how the head could grow back another tail, but I wonder if the tail half really knows how to grow back another head. Worms don't really have blood, but they do have guts. You can get them on your shirt.

I throw it as hard as I can out into the water and the bobber goes plop. Then you have to hold still and wait until a hungry fish sees the worm and bites it. When the fish bites it, the bobber goes underwater and you have to yank on the pole as hard as you can so the hook gets stuck in the fish's mouth. Daddy says fish don't have feelings either. Then I reel him in and Daddy takes him off the hook. Usually we catch sunnies but sometimes we catch a bass.

We throw the fishes back into the pond because Daddy doesn't like to clean fish and Mommy doesn't like to cook them.

One day when I want to go fishing, Daddy says, "No." He's tired from working. But I want to go fishing and it isn't fair. I can't have my fishing pole without Daddy, so I decide I'm going to make one. I have a bamboo pole Daddy gave me one time and I think I could make a fishing pole out of that like Huckleberry Finn. I know where we have string, so I cut a long string and tie it onto the end of the stick. I think about the hook. Daddy has a lot of them in his tackle box, but if I get one and he finds me, he's going to put it up where I can't reach it anymore. A safety pin looks a little bit like a hook and we have lots of those. I don't think you can catch a fish with a safety pin, but I guess you could pretend.

My fishing pole doesn't look so good and I don't have any worms. I take a shovel out of the barn and go down to the loading chute, but the dirt is hard as a rock. I stomp on the shovel as hard as I can like Daddy does, but it hurts through my shoes and doesn't make a hole.

So I just go fishing without any worms. I walk out onto the rock pile Daddy made for fishing and dip my hook in the water.

Up at the house Mommy and Daddy hear me start to scream and scream when the fish bites on my pole. I don't know what to do. I can't reel him in because I don't have a reel and he's a very strong fish. Daddy comes running down the bank from the house to the pond saying, "What's Going On?!" He can't believe I caught a fish on my pole. He didn't even know I made one.

I can't believe it either! Daddy pulls him in and he's a twelve-inch bass—the biggest fish I ever catch in our pond, ever in my whole life.

My tooth gets wiggly and loose. It gets more and more wiggly until it falls out and it doesn't even hurt. Mommy and Daddy say to put it under my pillow at night and the Tooth Fairy will give me a present. I ask what a Tooth Fairy is. Daddy says it's kind of like an angel that comes in the night when you're sleeping and takes the tooth out from under your pillow and leaves you a surprise. It must be a little surprise if it fits under your pillow. I don't think the Tooth Fairy is real, but Daddy says, "It is too. Try it and see."

I put my tooth under my pillow and sure enough in the morning there's a dime there and a stick of gum. I think Mommy did it.

Then my other tooth gets loose and it falls out too. Grandpa says I look like a jack'o lantern. It's too bad when your front teeth fall out in the summer like me because then you can't eat corn on the cob. Mommy has to cut it off and it's not as good cut off.

I decide I'm going to save all my teeth when they fall out, because after the Tooth Fairy gets them, she gives them to Mommy. Then when I'm big and in sixth grade and all my baby teeth fell out, I'm going to give them to my teacher. That will be a special present.

If me or Kelly are bad, sometimes Mommy makes us "sit on a chair." Sitting on a chair means you aren't going to get spanked, but if you do that again you might. It usually comes from fighting because if we back-talk we get smacked and if we disobey we get spanked. Mommy says, "Diana that's enough. You're going to have to sit on a chair until I tell you that you can get up."

Mommy always tells me what I did bad and what I'm supposed to think about while I'm sitting there—something like how Jesus wants us to be kind, or about patience or what to do besides getting into a fight. Mommy can make me sit on a chair, but she can't make me think anything. I think about what I feel like doing when I get off the chair. Sometimes she makes us sit there until we can say we're sorry. Sooner or later we have to say it even if we're not, or we could get spanked.

When you sit on a chair, Mommy pulls a kitchen chair out from the table into the middle of the kitchen and you have to sit there until she says, "You can get up now." You can't wiggle or make any noise. You have to sit like its church, and Mommy is watching while she works. She also makes sure nobody makes faces at the girl sitting on a chair.

Mommy sets the buzzer on the stove so she knows how long we sit there. She started doing that after she forgot about Kelly once and Kelly sat there for a very long time.

I have a Three Musketeers candy bar that Grandma Brubaker gave me. Kelly has one too so I don't have to share. I save it for a couple of days because I'm a big girl now. My Three Musketeers is lying on top of the toy box because I'm going to eat it today, but Mommy calls me into the kitchen. When I come back, Baby Michelle is standing up beside the toy box and she's eating my candy bar.

I scream for Mommy because Baby Michelle is eating my candy bar. It isn't fair. It's mine and I don't have to share it. She has chocolate on her face and she just looks at me and my candy bar is all slobbered up with baby slobber.

Sometimes I get mad at Kelly, but I never get *this* mad. I run into the kitchen and cry. The worst part is Mommy doesn't spank Baby Michelle like she would spank me—she takes a picture because Baby Michelle never stood up before. I don't know why we have to have Baby Michelle. That was my candy bar.

Mommy takes it away nicely and washes Baby Michelle's hands and face and says I can still have my candy bar. She says Baby Michelle only bit it a little and she can cut that part off. I don't want it anymore. She slobbered on the whole thing and it was mine and I didn't have to share it.

Mommy says I have to forgive her because she's just a baby and she doesn't understand. I know she's a baby and I don't care. I don't forgive her. That was my candy bar and *she* didn't care. She ruined it.

D addy says that the bumble bees with white dots on their faces can't sting. He says when he was a boy they used to catch them.

I want to catch one too, but I'm scared of bees. Also, what if you get the wrong kind? The bees with black faces can sting you and you have to be awfully close to a bee before you can see his face. I try to catch one but when I think I'm going to reach my hand out my legs run away.

When I'm big enough for first grade, I·have to get a lunchbox. Kelly gets to pick a book bag for kindergarten, but I have to use the same old one from last year because it isn't broken yet. We go to Rettews, down in the basement where they have children's things. It's hard to pick a lunchbox. Mommy doesn't like the ones about TV shows or Barbies and I don't want a dumb one with kitties or Mickey Mouse. I finally pick a blue one that's plastic and it has a funny-looking guy on the front and it says Rocky Roughneck. I don't know what that is, but it's better than the dumb pink ones that girls are supposed to pick.

Everybody at school laughs at my lunchbox and says, "Rocky Roughneck?! Who's Rocky Roughneck?"

I don't know. But at least it isn't pink.

In first grade, our teacher is Mrs. Chafin and she is very very nice. She doesn't get angry at us very often. She has some clowns on top of her cabinet to tell us when we're being naughty. If she tells us to be quiet and we don't, she goes over and gets down the clown with a sad face. She holds it up and we all know the clown is sad and Mrs. Chafin is sad because we aren't being good. If we keep on being noisy, she gets down the other clown with a *very very* sad face who is crying. When I see *that* clown, I want to cry too. That means we were very bad and the clown is crying because now Mrs. Chafin is going to have to punish us and make us miss five minutes of recess. She doesn't ever need to shout at us. We feel bad for those sad clowns.

I'm excited because finally I'm going to learn to read. I thought we were going to learn in kindergarten, but kindergarten was easy. I want to do homework.

All of us get a blue book called the "Tag Book" that teaches us how to write letters and what they say. The "Tag Book" has easy words like "tag" and "bag" and "it."

Hey. Does that mean I can read now?

The bus stop is at one of the houses at the top of the hill. Karen is lucky because it's close to her house. Mommy has to drive us to the bus stop and pick us up because it's too far away. Except sometimes when it's warm and sunny Mommy doesn't come. That means it's a nice day and we have to walk.

Walking all the way down the hill and in the lane takes a long, long time and I have to wait for Kelly. The lane is nice and I feel like a girl in a story from a long time ago who had to walk a long, long way to school. Everything in the meadow is buzzing and chirping. The only problem with walking home is that I get very, very hungry. We always get to have a snack when we get home and walking takes a lot longer than driving. Daddy puts a squirrel house in one of the trees along the lane and he tells us that if we ever see a squirrel go in or out he will take us to Twin Kiss for ice-cream cones. We always look up at the squirrel house, but we never see a squirrel--not even a tail. We think about saying we did, but that would be lying.

In the barn, there is "The Shop" where Daddy keeps his tools. He fixes the tractors when they break. He has hammers and nails and screws and saws and screwdrivers and wrenches and pliers and things I don't know what they are. There's a thing called a vise-grip that I like. I put wood in it and then I can make the vise-grip hold onto it tight by twisting its hands together. I like to saw the wood in the vise-grip and then pound nails into it. Maybe when I'm big I could be a carpenter. I never heard of a lady carpenter, but I guess I could be one.

One day I find a bottle of blue powder. Its beautiful bright blue like the sky and it smells like chalk. I pour some out and spread it around. It's so pretty. It gets on my hands, but that's ok, I can wash them. I decorate Daddy's shop in the barn with beautiful blue.

"That blue chalk isn't for pretty. It's for making straight lines," Daddy tells me and he isn't happy to see it everywhere and all over me. He tells me not to play with it anymore and puts it up so high I don't know how he got it up there. And I don't think he knows how to get it back down because he never does.

There's a man at church that me and Kelly are scared of. His name is Ron Burkhart and he's Daddy's friend. Ron Burkhart doesn't have any little girls; he only has little boys, so he likes to see us in our Sunday dresses. Ron Burkhart is a nice man, but he tickles too much. Mommy says he's trying to play with us, but he doesn't know when to stop. That sure is true. Ron Burkhart catches us and tickles us until we're screaming and can't breathe and he doesn't notice that we're not laughing anymore and we're really almost crying.

Mommy and Daddy don't like it either, but he's a big man and they can't tell him what to do. They tell us just not to go too close to him so he can't reach us.

Daddy gets a box in the mail. It has holes in it and it's full of baby ducks. Who would have thought you could get a box of ducks in the mail? Daddy says he ordered them so they can grow up and live in the pond. He makes them a special pen in the barn with shavings from the chicken house and chicken feed and water.

I love the duckies. I go up into the barn and watch them. I get into the pen and play with them. They are just like baby chicks but with bigger feet and bigger beaks.

I think about those baby ducks and how they don't have a mommy. The mommy duck has to teach the baby ducks important things and these duckies don't have a mommy to teach them. I learn a lot about animals on *Wild Kingdom*. I know how ducks dive down underwater to eat things down there. These duckies eat chicken feed, they don't know about diving underwater to look for things.

I decide to teach them. There's bucket of water beside their pen and I put them into the water. They like that and they swim around saying, "Peep, peep." I push one under water and it pops back up. I push it down again like the teacher did to me in swimming lessons so it learns to hold its breath like I did.

The duckies do a good job and when they get tired and don't want to swim anymore, I lay them down in their pen so they can sleep.

Daddy says he can't believe I drowned his ducks.

I wasn't drowning them, I was helping them. I was teaching them. I like them, I don't want them to die. I thought they were tired from swimming. The duckies are all dead and Daddy says I did it. Now I want to cry when I think about the duckies because I was going to name them and go swimming with them in the pond and be their friend. I can't believe I made them die, all of them.

All my whole life Daddy says, "I can't believe Diana drowned my ducks!" All my whole life I can't believe it either. I wish he forgot about that and didn't say it anymore.

I have a bad dream about the house catching on fire.

We learn about fires at school. We see filmstrips and movies about how to prevent fires and how to be safe from fires. Your house can catch on fire at night while you're sleeping and, if you don't wake up, you could burn up. Especially if your house is old and wood like ours. All your things will burn up, and if you can't find everyone in your family, they could burn up. Fires are very dangerous and they can even happen when you aren't at home. You could come home from church and your house could be all burned up. If your mommy doesn't come to pick you up, it could be because she burned up in your house.

I have a lot of bad dreams. I have bad dreams every night and I don't want to go to sleep.

We get books at school about how to make your house safe from fires and about how firemen look for special stickers on the windows where children are sleeping. We get a sticker for our window. I don't know what to do because me and Kelly have our room together now but what about Baby Michelle? What if the fireman saves us and Baby Michelle burns up? But if I put a sticker on her window, they might not know there are more children, and me and Kelly could burn up. I decide to cut it and put half of it on each window so the firemen will know to look in both rooms.

Also, I'm very scared about Mommy and Daddy. I ask them who will take care of us if they burn up and they say they aren't going to burn up, God is taking care of us. Well, some people burn up and God is supposed to take care of everyone. I'm very scared.

Our book says we need to have a meeting place for if there's a fire so we can know if anyone is still inside. Daddy says we can meet in the yard and he tries to make me stop being scared. It doesn't help. Our book says everyone has to sleep with their doors closed because, if there's a fire, everybody could be dead from smoke before they even wake up.

Mommy gets very angry at the teacher and takes my fire book away and says it's terrible to talk about these things with children. When I'm at school Mommy calls her and tells her.

Mice can run fast, but I can run faster and I catch one by the tail. I see him in the lane when I'm walking home from school. I know that mice can bite, so I catch him by the tail and carry him home upside down. He doesn't like it and he wiggles a lot, but I tell him it's ok, I'm not going to hurt him. I talk to him all the way home and give him a name and plan how I'm going to tame him. He's going to be my pet mouse and his name is Gus.

Mommy and Daddy would never buy me a mouse, but I caught this one all by myself. He's mine and they can't take him away from me. He likes me. I decide I'm going to make him a nice mouse house in a bucket with grass and water and some wire on top so the kitties can't eat him.

When I get home, I go straight to the barn to get a bucket for Gus. He doesn't try to get out—he just sits there. He knows I'm going to be nice to him. I know Mommy always screams at mice so I don't bring him inside. I say, "Mommy, look what I caught."

She comes outside and says, "*OOOOOOGH!*"

She doesn't like Gus. Daddy doesn't either. He says Gus is sick and makes me wash my hands with Lava soap.

I say, "No, he isn't sick."

Daddy says the kitties will eat him.

I say I will keep him safe.

Daddy says if that mouse wasn't sick, I couldn't have caught him, and I can't have a sick mouse—mice carry sicknesses and can make you sick.

But I like Gus and he likes me and I caught him.

Daddy can see I'm going to cry and he makes me put him in the barn. We put wire on the top with a stone on it so the kitties can't get my mouse.

I go to see Gus in the morning and the bucket is lying over on the floor and Gus isn't in it. Mommy and Daddy say they guess a kitty knocked it over trying to eat Gus and he ran away.

Now we have special classes. We have Art Class and Music Class and Gym Class. For Gym Class, we get to go outside when it's not too cold, and when it is too cold, we have Gym in the kindergarten room in the morning before the little kids come. Our Gym teacher is Mr. DiAngelo but we're allowed to call him Mr. D because that's a hard name. He's nice and we play fun games. Mr. D always wears pants with a stripe on the side. On Gym day, I wear a culotte skirt so everyone won't see my panties.

The Art teacher is Mr. Condract. We don't get to go outside for Art, but we do get to talk to our friends and walk around a little. We make things out of paper and paints and crayons and tracing and cutting. Mr. Condract always has a good idea for things to make. He's a little mean, though, if we make too much noise, and we sometimes call him Count Dracula because it sounds like Condract. Count Dracula is a monster.

Some of the boys and girls don't like Music, but I do. Mrs. Meyers comes to our room and teaches songs to us. I love singing and I like new songs. Some people are embarrassed to sing, but not me. I'm used to singing because our family sings up front at church sometimes. Sometimes we even go to sing at other people's churches. My favorite one is *God Told Jonah,* but we don't sing that one at school.

Daddy gets me a bike from Mel Stutzman that Denise used to ride when she was little. It has training wheels on it and I can ride it good. When there aren't any chickens in the chicken houses, we can ride in there; Kelly rides her tricycle and Michelle rides her Big Wheel. The chicken houses are big and you can go really fast because there aren't any bumps like when you ride in the lane.

Then Daddy takes the training wheels off. I want them back on because I don't know how to ride it with the training wheels off. Daddy says I'm big enough to learn to ride a bike without training wheels and I want to but I'm scared. I don't know how.

Daddy holds onto the back and I'm scared he will let go. He says he won't. He tells me to go and to turn the way I feel like I'm going to fall. But I can't. I'm scared. Daddy says, "Yes, you can," and makes me keep trying. Then I see what he means about turning the way you fall, but I'm always falling and turning every which way and that's not right! Daddy says I'm doing good.

Then Daddy tells me I'm doing it by myself and he isn't holding on to me anymore. As soon as he says that I fall over.

But now I know how to do it all by myself. Daddy has to hold me up when I start going and I fall off when I have to stop, but in the middle I can ride.

We aren't allowed to say "gosh" or "golly" or "gee," because those words sound like God and Jesus and they are making fun of them and taking their names in vain. Some of the kids in school say "darn." I think about "darn." That doesn't sound like anybody's name. Mommy doesn't say it, but maybe Mommy doesn't know it.

One day at home I say "darn," and Mommy jumps straight up and snaps me hard on the forehead with her finger and says, "We don't say that word at our house."

I almost cry because Mommy scares me and I didn't even know it was a bad word. My head hurts where she snapped me. I ask why because I think it only sounds like barn. She says because it means damn, which is a *very very* bad word I would never say and I can't believe Mommy just said it. She tells me it means going to hell. I didn't know that. I bet the boys and girls at school who say it don't know that either.

Great Grandma Neff gets sick and dies because she is very old. She's Mommy's grandma and Grandma's mommy. I would be very sad if my Grandma or my Mommy died, but Grandma Neff is really old and it's ok for her to die because she's with Jesus now. Mommy isn't going to take us to the funeral, but I say I want to go. I never went to a funeral before.

We all wear Sunday dresses and go to the church. We look at Grandma Neff lying in a casket and she looks like she's sleeping. I never saw a dead person before. She looks normal except she's lying so still. I wonder who got her dressed after she was dead. Somebody combed her hair and made her look nice. Mommy doesn't cry, but Grandma cries a little. I wonder what's going to happen when my mommy dies. Everybody has to die sometime. I hope I'm an old lady like Grandma when Mommy dies. It's very dark and quiet and there are a lot of old people and flowers. I wonder if the old people are scared when they see Great Grandma Neff dead in her casket. I would be. They're probably going to die soon too and all their friends will come and look at them.

I know that when we die we go to be with Jesus and I know in heaven everyone is happy forever, but I don't want to die and I don't want people I know to die either. Maybe Jesus will come back while I'm still alive and then I won't have to die. But I hope he waits until I'm old because if he comes back now, I'll never get to find out what I'm going to be when I grow up.

Daddy goes to Canada and shoots a moose. He brings me a yellow shirt with a picture of a moose on it too. We eat moose meat and Daddy gets its head and we put it in the living room. The moose is very big; much bigger than Daddy's deer heads. It has big horns and its eyes are made of marbles and we can't touch it.

When Donna Wenger comes to baby sit us, she walks into the living room and, when she sees the moose head in the dark, she screams very loud. Then she starts crying even though she's big and she has to call her mommy on the telephone.

Me and Kelly think it's funny. We're not scared of that moose head! It isn't even alive.

I love the Manheim Parade. We have to wear our coats and hoods and mittens because it's cold at night and we drive in the car to Manheim.

Trucks drive by slow and honk their horns and the drivers are waving at us and they throw candy into the street, or gum or pencils and things. Then you run out and get them. Marching bands come by blowing their horns and pounding their drums so loud my heart almost stops. I'm scared of the people in the bands because they're all dressed up like soldiers and some of them even have things that look like guns. Mommy says they aren't soldiers but they look like soldiers and they march like soldiers and look mean. There's horses too and floats where people are waving and throwing candy. I love the parade. Some of the people in it we know, like Cousin Earl is driving a big truck and he blows the horn and waves at me. Yolanda from school rides her horse.

My favorite part is the baton twirlers. They look like ballet dancers in their tights and silvery skirts and their hair put up. They throw their batons up and catch them and spin around and dance and look so beautiful. I wish I had a baton. I want to be a baton twirler.

Mommy and Daddy say, "No." The baton twirlers are marching down the street in swimsuits, they say, and that's immodest. We don't do that.

Kathy Metzler's allowed. They go to a Mennonite church too, like us. Mommy and Daddy say they aren't responsible for Kathy—that her mommy and daddy are and if she was their little girl she would not be in baton twirling. I wish I was in Kathy Metzler's family.

At Christmas, there are special lights in Manheim. They are the prettiest lights in the world. There is a giant Christmas tree in the middle of the square that reaches out over the whole town and stretches way up into the sky. Daddy drives around under it and we look up at the amazing green and red lights going by. The middle of it is up in the stars.

When I get sick, I have to stay home from school so the other boys and girls don't get it. I don't like missing school but sometimes I have to and I guess it's kind of fun to stay home. I come downstairs and lie on the sofa in the living room with the soft pillow from my bed and Mommy covers me. I get to lie there all day and eat saltines and drink 7UP. We never get to have 7UP unless we're sick. We get to watch TV a little bit too. The news is on a long time and then *Captain Kangaroo* and I watch him just like in the summer. Phil Donahue comes on and Mommy lets that on sometimes until people start arguing too much.

If my belly is sick, Mommy puts a dishpan on the floor beside me so I can throw up into it. She comes and feels my head and takes my temperature and sometimes gives me special things to do or play with. When I start getting better, I can have toast and dippy-eggs.

If you're sick on Sunday, you don't have to go to church and Mommy or Daddy stays home with you. It feels funny being home on Sunday. The house feels different and quiet. Everybody else is in church and you're not, but God can see you're sick so it's alright.

I like being sick on Sunday. It's fun to stay home from church when the house feels funny. I get to watch more TV programs then, too—especially if Daddy stays home because he likes the TV more than Mommy. If Daddy stays home with me, sometimes he keeps the TV on the whole time straight until *Call of the Outdoors,* even if cartoons come on. Mommy never does that.

A ll my friends at school watch cartoons on Saturday morning and we're not allowed. It's not fair. Cartoons are funny, they aren't bad. Mommy says, "No." She says, "We have better things to do." She says, "They're too stupid."

How does she know if she never watches them? She says people who watch too much TV start to think those things are real. No, they don't. Nobody thinks Bugs Bunny and Mickey Mouse are real! Mommy is too stupid if she thinks that.

Mommy and Daddy decide to change our house. They have special papers that are very big called a "Blue Print" that they put on the kitchen table and look at with men who come over. They won't let us girls put even one finger on the Blue Print because it's so important.

Daddy gets a trailer and puts it out by the chicken house that is "House 2," and we're going to live in there until the house is finished remodeling. House 2 has a telephone in the feed room so we can hear it ringing if somebody calls us.

I love the trailer! I always wanted to live in a trailer. I ask Mommy and Daddy if we can keep it and they say, "No." They say they used to live in a trailer before I was born and then when I was a tiny baby. I remember a lot of things, but I don't remember that.

The trailer has a kitchen and a living room that are like one big room. We bring our table and chairs and sofa and the TV and a lot of our things from the house. We bring our mattresses from our beds and put them on the floor so it's almost like going camping. We bring our dollies and our books and our clothes. Daddy brings his guitar and his banjo. Maybe when I grow up I can get a trailer and put it here beside House 2. Daddy brings the swing set over and puts it right beside the trailer and we love it!

Men come and work on the house. They tear down the washhouse and the kitchen and they cover up the walk and make the hill different. It doesn't look like our house anymore. They tear off Mommy and Daddy's bedroom and the downstairs bathroom. We aren't allowed to go over there because it's very very dangerous. Now there aren't any walls and you can look right into our house!

150

They leave my room there, and the spare room and Kelly's room and the upstairs bathroom. Daddy says they're going to make the house bigger. I thought our house was big enough, but I guess it's okay as long as I can still have my own room and I don't have to share with Kelly anymore.

In second grade, Mrs. Mentzer is the teacher and sometimes she is mean. She isn't always mean like Mrs. Eberly the fourth-grade teacher, but she isn't always nice like Mrs. Chafin.

Mrs. Mentzer is mean and gets me into trouble all the time for talking. I don't think she likes me very much. She thinks I'm bad. I try not to be bad, but Mrs. Mentzer is always angry at me. Every time Karen or Kathy or Mike Travis talks to me I get into trouble and not them.

I spill the blue paint on the new yellow dress Mommy made me and I start to cry because it's my new dress. Then Mrs. Mentzer yells at me because I spilled paint on my dress. A lot of paint. Then I cry more because Mrs. Mentzer is yelling at me.

I don't know why she has to be so mean to me when I'm already crying. If I tried it, I wouldn't be crying—I would be laughing. She's mean to me while she tries to help me get it off and she says, "What is your mother going to say?" Mrs. Mentzer tells me my mommy is going to be very mad at me for ruining my new dress. I have to go home on the bus with a big blue wet spot on my new dress and everyone can see I'm crying.

Mommy is very mad, but not at me. She says she knows it was an accident and that's okay—accidents happen and we'll wash my dress and I can still wear it if I want. Mommy is mad at Mrs. Mentzer for being mean to me when I was already sorry. Mommy doesn't think you should yell at children and neither do I.

The big blue spot never comes off my yellow dress, but I wear it anyway for Everyday. I like it and besides, who cares about a blue spot? It doesn't have any holes in it and it still fits me so it *isn't* ruined.

When the men fixing our house are fixing the living room, they find a hole in the ceiling that goes up under my bed. They move away the linoleum on the floor and I can see all the way down into the living room. Me and Kelly make up a game where we bring things up and down through the hole by tying a string on them.

Mommy and Daddy say it's a stovepipe hole from the old days when people used to have wood stoves. I like my stovepipe hole and I want to keep it, but Mommy and Daddy say, "No." They have to cover it up. We can't have a hole in our house.

We have ducks and geese that swim in the pond. The ducks are nice, but I don't like the geese. The geese are called African Geese. They're white and gray, very big and very mean. If we get near them, they put their heads way down at the ground and stretch their necks out flat and say "Sssssss" really mean. And if you don't run away, they run at you. And if you don't run fast enough, they chase you.

I don't know why they're so mean. Nothing you can do ever makes them stop being mean. Daddy says they're mean because they're afraid of us. The ducks are afraid of us too and the ducks aren't mean. I wish we didn't have geese. Mommy and Daddy think they're pretty. Every year the girl goose lays eggs. They never hatch though, which is good because we don't need any more geese! If they get you, they bite you hard and flap you with their wings.

I go fishing by myself and I'm standing on the row of rocks that stretches out into the pond catching fish. The geese come down from the barn and come right over to the rocks. I'm scared because they are standing in the grass beside the rocks and I'm at the other end in the water. I tell them to go away and I try to act like I'm not scared.

I am very scared. They honk at me and say "Sssssss" with their necks down.

I'm trapped and I call for Mommy and Daddy. They're inside and they can't hear me. I can't jump into the water because it's too cold and it's deep at the end of the rocks. I stop fishing and start crying because the geese are going to get me and there is no one to help me. I knew they were going to get me someday and now they caught me where I'm trapped.

I scream for Mommy as loud as I can. She comes out onto the porch and tells me, "You're all right. They won't hurt you."

Yes, they *will* hurt me. Mommy is big and they won't hurt *her*, but I'm little.

I scream and cry more and the geese say "Sssssssss."

Mommy calls to me and says if I come back off the rocks, they will go away.

No, they won't. They will bite me and flop me because I can't run away. I hate the geese and I keep on screaming.

Finally, Mommy has to get her shoes on and come save me from the geese. When Mommy comes down from the house and hollers at them, they go honking away and I can come off the rocks and they can't get me.

I don't know why we have to have geese. It isn't fair. Geese are dangerous to little girls.

Some of the big kids on the bus are selling candy bars for Girl Scouts and Boy Scouts. They have caramel ones and crunch ones and ones with nuts. They cost fifty cents.

I tell Mommy I want money to buy one, but Mommy says fifty cents is too much for a candy bar. But they're big candy bars! Then she says that's too much candy.

I tell her it's for Girl Scouts and Boy Scouts.

Mommy says we don't give money to Girl Scouts and Boy Scouts because they teach you to love the government more than God and then you could become a soldier when you grow up and kill people.

I can't believe Girl and Boy Scouts are bad *too*.

She says, "We give our money to God in the offering at Church."

But we don't get candy bars for the offering. I say please so many times she finally says, "Yes."

I pick caramel because that's my favorite. It's the best candy bar in the world. I want another one, but Mommy says, "No more," even though all the other kids are allowed to have them.

One day when Mommy isn't looking, I take two quarters from her wallet. I just want one more. I pick caramel again, but I have to hide in my seat when I eat it so Kelly doesn't see me because Kelly will tell.

Then I get worried because I guess I stole. Like the time I gave Jeremy five dollars. Now the only way to be sure I'm not going to go to hell is to confess it to God and to Mommy and ask them to forgive me.

Mommy will forgive me, but first she'll spank me because I know better and I did it anyway. I decide I can confess it to God and tell him I'm sorry now because God's the most important. Then, when I'm twenty, I can confess it to Mommy. Twenty is too big to spank. If I die first or Jesus comes back, he probably won't send me to hell if he knows I really *am* sorry and I was *going* to confess it.

Me and Kelly go home on bus 16. Bus 16 is the best bus. At the end of the day, the teacher calls out the numbers of the buses and all the people on that bus have to get into their line. Bus 16 has a very long line. We walk in rows out to our buses and wave goodbye to all the teachers. Our bus driver's name is Lazer Shenk and he knows Grandpa Brubaker. Lazer is a funny name.

The little kids have to sit in the front and the big kids can sit in the back. We have to stay in our seats and stay turned around and we can't shout. There's a bus Patrolman that's in sixth grade and wears an orange belt with a badge. I'm scared of the Patrolman because he looks like a policeman and, if you're bad, he can report you.

The bus seats have metal bars across the back part and you can hold onto the one in front of you if you want.

I put my top teeth onto the bar to feel the bumping and it feels funny. Then Lazer goes over a bump and I break a little piece off my front tooth. It doesn't hurt, but it was my big tooth so I guess that piece isn't ever going to grow back.

My favorite cousin is Doris. She's Uncle Nelson's girl and she has David, who is twins with her. Doris is bigger than me, but we like to play. Mommy and Daddy have to go away for a few days and I pick Doris' house to go stay at. At Doris' house, I can only wear dresses because that's what their church believes in, not even culotte skirts. I don't care because its summer and me a Doris have bare feet and dresses and long pigtails the same.

Uncle Nelson and Aunt Mary Ann are a lot meaner than Mommy and Daddy. Doris and David and John and Karen all have to be quiet at the table and no one laughs. When Uncle Nelson tells somebody to do something they better not forget! We have to mind Mommy and Daddy too, but they aren't mad at us unless we're naughty on purpose. At Uncle Nelson and Aunt Mary Ann's house, you better not be naughty by accident either. Maybe that's why Doris is so quiet.

Doris is lucky because she has brothers. I wish I had brothers, especially big brothers. John isn't very much fun but at least he's a big brother and besides, she has David too. We play fun things outside and in the barn and we play Hide and Seek upstairs until Aunt Mary Ann makes us go outside for that too.

My favorite thing to do at Doris' house is watch for parachutes. We lie in the grass on the hill in front of her house and watch for airplanes in the sky. The big airplanes are up too high and just make white lines where they go. The little airplanes are the ones people jump out of. I want to jump with a parachute someday. I would be scared, but it would be fun. If your parachute doesn't open up, you die, but I think they always open up. Me and Doris lie there and watch them float around. Uncle Nelson has a little airplane he flies, but they don't have any parachutes. I can't imagine any of them doing that. Besides, you can't go parachute jumping in a dress or everyone in the world will see your panties.

160

Me and Doris get into trouble because its nighttime and we keep on giggling and whispering. Then we laugh because we are trying not to make any noise. Aunt Mary Ann tells us to be quiet, but she still hears us and when she comes back again, she's angry already and makes us sleep in different beds. I like Doris but now I feel sorry for her. Usually when Mommy and Daddy come to get me I don't want to go home, but this time I do.

My other cousins I like to play with from Daddy's brothers are Mitchell and Melvin. They're littler than me and Melvin is littler than Kelly and then they have Becky, who is a baby like Michelle. Uncle Paul is their daddy and Aunt Donna is their mommy and she is very fat. They live in Potter County near the mountains where Daddy likes to go hunting.

We jump on the beds because Aunt Donna isn't mean like Aunt Mary Ann and we scream and run around outside and play with the dogs and we love it.

It takes a long time to drive to their house. One day, while we're on the way there in the car, I learn how to whistle. I've been trying for the longest time and all I do is blow air. Then it just comes out and I can do it.

All of the sudden we can't play with Mitchell and Melvin anymore because Uncle Paul and Aunt Donna decide to go do a different church that doesn't let you do anything. They can't have musical instruments or nice toys or radios and they have to wear long sleeves all year long and they can't run around screaming and laughing anymore. They have to be serious. And boys aren't allowed to play with girls.

I don't understand why anyone would want to change to a church like that. Mommy says Uncle Paul got scared of the world. I don't see why. Now I'm scared of Uncle Paul. I don't think Jesus wants us to be serious all the time and Mommy and Daddy don't either. I'm sad and Mommy and Daddy are very sad. So we don't visit Uncle Paul much anymore, and when we do Mitchell and Melvin get into trouble every time we do something fun. I'm glad my Daddy didn't decide *we* have to go to that kind of church. And I hope he never does.

It isn't fair that when it's hot, Daddy and Michelle don't have to wear shirts. Daddy doesn't have to wear one because he's a man and Michelle doesn't have to wear one because she's little. It's so hot I think I'm going to die. It's even hot in front of the fan.

I ask Mommy if I can take my shirt off too. Mommy says, "No."

I say but it isn't fair; Daddy doesn't have to wear a shirt and Michelle doesn't either.

Mommy says that's different—that I'm a big girl and big girls wear shirts.

I am not a big girl. I'm eight and I don't have any breasts and it's hot.

Mommy says, "Because I said so."

But it isn't *fair*. I have to die of heat because I'm a girl. I tell them it's not fair and I *will* wear a shirt when I'm big and have breasts. There aren't any other people here—just us.

Daddy says, "Don't you back-talk to your mother."

I say well if I have to wear one, then Daddy and Michelle do too.

Daddy says if I can't remember who's in charge around here, he'll have to help me. Help means spank.

It isn't fair and Mommy and Daddy don't care about me. I can't do anything I want to. Now I'm hot *and* mad *and* I have to be quiet. I hope I have a little girl someday. I won't make her wear anything.

Frank and Harold are the carpenters making our new house and they're my friends. Every day I go talk to them. I tell them lots of stories while they work and I tell them about the things I dream because dreams are funny. Mommy and Daddy tell me not to bother them, but I'm not bothering them. I'm just talking to them.

I make them a present so they can see what a nice, smart little girl I am and that, even though I'm a girl, I can hammer good. There are lots of extra pieces of wood and I think of something I could make them that they can use: a flyswatter. I find a nice square of wood and a stick for a handle. I go to the shop and nail them together with Daddy's nails. I don't even hit my thumb.

They say, "thank you" when I give it to them and they think it should work pretty good for killing flies.

Frank gives me a present. He says he's going to make me a necklace of chicken teeth.

I say chickens don't have teeth.

He says, "Did you ever look?"

I guess I didn't, but Daddy says they don't and Daddy knows everything about chickens. He says they don't need teeth because they have beaks. I think maybe Frank is going to make me a chicken beak necklace.

He doesn't. It's pretty, made of different colors of wire and beads. I'm not allowed to wear necklaces, but Mommy lets me wear the one Frank made me as long as I wear it only at home and nobody is coming over. It doesn't have anything from chickens on it.

D addy can play the guitar and the banjo. Mommy can play the piano and the accordion. I know what I want to play. I want to play the drums. The drums feel like they're thumping right inside your heart. Piano music and guitar music are nice, but everybody plays them and I want to play something special. Besides, it looks easy.

I tell Mommy and Daddy I want to play the drums and they say, "No." They say we don't play the drums because drums are what they play in rock music and that comes from Satan and the drums come from the jungles where people worship the Devil.

I think about this. I don't want to be sinful, but drums don't seem sinful to me. They're just drums. I'm not going to play rock music— anyway, I don't even know any rock music songs. I can sing *Father Abraham* and *This Land Is Your Land*. I tell Mommy and Daddy I won't play rock music. I tell them I love God, not the Devil.

I ask for a drum set so many times that finally they get me one. It has Mickey Mouse all over it so no one would ever think it's real, but I don't care. Up until now we never had Mickey Mouse at our house, either. Mommy and Daddy tell me I can have it in the basement and play it all I want, but I am not going to be allowed to play the drums anywhere else *ever* (like at school) and I can't play them for Grandma.

I play the drums until they are all broken. By that time, I am big enough to know that I'm a good drummer but Mommy and Daddy would never let me. So I don't ask for any more drums and I never play them again. But I want to.

There's a lot of things we can play outside at recess. There's monkey bars and a jungle gym on one side of the school and there's four-square and hopscotch painted on the ground. The other side has grass and over there we can play kickball. Mostly boys play kickball and the girls play on the other things.

There are a lot of things to play on! There's a sliding board and swings and a merry-go-round and see-saws. I like the swings the best but we aren't allowed to swing upside down or hang on our bellies if the teachers are looking. The sliding board is very big and mostly only the big boys and girls go down it. I like the see-saws too. Sometimes we put two girls on each side so that we can go up and down faster.

We have a see-saw game called "Farmer Farmer Let Me Down." How you play it is you don't let the other person come down and so they have to say "Farmer, Farmer let me down." Then you say, "What will you give me?" Then they have to think of things like a candy bar or all the ice cream in the world or Matthew or Jeremy or gold or silver or something. You can say "no" and don't let them down until they think of something you want. Then it's your turn to go up and think of things.

I watch people doing gymnastics on TV and I want to do that. They do flips and splits and cartwheels and all kinds of hard things. Jennifer Brown and Vicki Henderson go to gymnastics class and I want to too.

I tell Mommy I want to take gymnastics.

Mommy says, "No."

I tell Daddy I want to take gymnastics. Daddy and Mommy talk about it and they say, "No."

I cry because I *really* want to take gymnastics.

They say no daughter of theirs is going to go around in public in a swimming suit like that; it's immodest and we don't do that at our house. It's okay for other people, but not for us.

I don't understand why. There's only girls in gymnastics. Even if I'm really good at it, I won't let them put me on TV. I tell them I could wear a culotte skirt.

They say, "No."

I don't want to be naughty; I want to learn to do handsprings and flips.

They say, "No," and if I don't stop carrying on I'm going to get spanked.

I decide that they can make me not go to gymnastics class, but they can't make me not learn. I watch the girls on TV and I watch Jennifer and Vicki at school. I practice in the yard and in the living room. Mommy and Daddy don't mind about that. I learn to do everything the girls in gymnastics do and everybody says, "You should take gymnastics."

I know. I think so too.

Mommy says I have to take piano lessons. I don't want to take piano lessons. All little girls take piano lessons—I want to play something else. Mommy says I have to take piano lessons first and then if I want to I can take other lessons. I want to take drum lessons, but I know I can't. I want to play the guitar like Daddy, but my hands are too little. I want to play the trumpet like the angels, but you can't take instrument lessons at my school until you're in third grade and I'm only in 2nd. Mommy says if I take piano lessons this year, I can take trumpet lessons next year.

My piano teacher is a big fat lady with a piano in a room so little she can hardly shut the door. She makes me sit up straight and hold my hands a certain way. I have to play dumb stupid baby songs. Sometimes I like the songs I have to practice, but mostly I don't. I think enough girls know how to play the piano and I don't care if I never learn. I would rather play the banjo.

Mommy lets me stop taking piano lessons from that lady and get another teacher when she tells me I'm getting fat. That wasn't very nice and anyway nobody in the world is fatter than her!

When our house is all done, we move back in. It doesn't feel like the old house. It echoes because it's empty. The living room doesn't have any carpet in it yet, just cardboard on the floor. I like the cardboard floor because we can color on it. We make hopscotch and four-square like at school and its fun. I wish we didn't have to get carpet.

Now there's enough bedrooms to each have one plus the spare room. Since I'm the biggest, I get to pick first and I can have any room I want besides Mommy and Daddy's room. There's a new room beside Mommy and Daddy's room that's the biggest with two doors and two closets and I can have it if I want. It has carpet and new paint. My old room has the same old green and yellow linoleum and the same ugly green walls. The walls are even uglier now because the workers painted white on the cracks and left it that way. Plus, the new room has heaters in it and my old room doesn't. But the new room only has one tiny window in it so you have to turn the lights on in there even in the day. My old room is little and it has three great big windows in it with windowsills. I can see the pond and the lane and my tree and all the fields. I can see the moon from my bed at night.

I keep my old room with the ugly walls and the pretty windows.

On Saturdays, we have radio programs we listen to in the kitchen while we color or make cookies. First Uncle Charlie comes on. It says, "It's time for the *Children's Bible Hour with Uncle Charlie,*" then everyone sings *Boys And Girls For Jesus, This Our Earnest Prayer...* Uncle Charlie has songs and stories about children who are bad and then bad things happen to them and they learn their lesson about following God.

Next comes Ranger Bill. Ranger Bill is a Christian program too, but it's funnier than Uncle Charlie. Stumpy is a funny old man who says "You Whipper-Snapper," and sometimes he's grumpy. They say, "Ranger Bill, Warrior of the Woodland!" I love Ranger Bill. I wish girls could be rangers. Maybe I could be one anyway.

Uncle Charlie always tells us that we should tell all our friends about Jesus because if they don't know about Jesus and they die, they have to go to hell. He says it's our job to do that. In Sunday School, the teacher tells us too that if we love Jesus, we should tell our friends at school about him. I think about this. Most of my friends know about Jesus, I think. But if some of them don't, they could go to hell, and it would be my fault. I could even go to hell too because I know I was supposed to tell them and I didn't.

I ask them.

Michelle Evans doesn't go to church and neither does Missy Snider or Glenn. Glenn is in Kelly's class and everyone picks on him. I tell them we're going to have a Bible Club at lunch recess.

I bring my book of Bible stories and we sit on the roots of the big tree on the side of the playground and I read to them. Missy Snider doesn't come because she's a little bit bad, but Glenn and Michelle come. They've never even heard of Adam and Eve, so I start in the beginning when God makes the world. No use telling them about Jesus if they don't even know about God.

The teachers find out about Bible Club and they tell Mommy and Mommy makes me stop. She says that Uncle Charlie is wrong about children; that children can't go to hell. She seems a little bit mad at Uncle Charlie because she can tell I'm scared that Michelle and Glenn might go to hell and me too.

Mommy says that it's Michelle and Glenn's parents' job to teach them and that my job is to be a good example of Jesus' love. She said Jesus wants me to be nice to them and love them like he does and don't be afraid of hell because all children belong to God. He said, "Let the little children come to Me."

I wonder when you get big enough to go to hell. Mommy says it's when you reach "The Age of Accountability" and that's different for everybody. I wish it were a set age so you would know. That way if I wanted to do something naughty, I would do it before then.

In the summer, when it's hot, sometimes Daddy puts the pup tent up in the yard. The pup tent isn't a pup—it's a tent. It doesn't even look like a pup—it's just very little.

Only two people can sleep in the pup tent, so Daddy sleeps out in the yard with me one night and with Kelly the next night. Mommy doesn't like sleeping in the yard. I put my jammies on like always and Mommy gets some sleeping bags and sheets and Daddy makes our beds. We each get to have flashlights under our pillows and we put bug spray on for the mosquitoes.

It's hot when we go to sleep but when I wake up in the middle of the night, it's a little cold and everything is all wet. The grass is very wet. You can hear the crickets and peepers and bullfrogs. The house looks big and black with all its lights off. Daddy snores loud and he won't stop until I wiggle all around and make a lot of noise and he rolls over.

The best thing we ever do is go to Spruce Lake. Spruce Lake is a camp, but we don't camp and we don't really even go to the lake.

I *love* Spruce Lake. I wish we could live there. It's three hours away, which is really far, so we pack up a lot of clothes and stay for a whole week. We also pack bags of things to do in the car because we have to sit there for THREE HOURS. We bring books and coloring books and crayons and snacks and dollies and everything because it's so far away. We aren't allowed to ask, "Are we there soon?" We are NOT there soon. I hope heaven is like Spruce Lake.

Spruce Lake has a heated pool. This doesn't mean it's hot water; it means it's warm water, even in the morning when the pool opens. We stay in that pool all day long. It has a shallow end and a deep end, a diving board and a sliding board that goes in a curve.

When we first go to Spruce Lake, I'm still taking swimming lessons. I think I can swim but really I still can't. I almost drown in that pool, but Mel Martin saves me. I'm playing and talking and all of a sudden, the floor isn't under me, only more water. I can't reach up and I can't reach down and I don't have any more air to blow bubbles like the fat swimming teacher taught us. I'm kicking and wiggling and I think it's a shame I'm going to be dead already because I'm still a little girl, when somebody pulls me up into the air and it's Mel Martin, Johnny's daddy. Mel Martin is Daddy's friend. He saves me from drowning and gives me to Daddy. I sit on the side of the pool for a little while until I feel better and then I start swimming again.

In the pool at Spruce Lake, Daddy teaches me how to dive. I can swim now, but when I try to dive, it smacks my belly.

Daddy tells me to squat at the edge with my knees apart. He shows me how to put my arms straight down and put my head between my arms. He says, "Now fall in head first."

I try and try, but I keep smacking my belly.

Daddy laughs and I laugh but I can't do it. I'm not scared, I just *can't*.

Then Daddy gets a good idea. He puts me on his back like piggy-back and he squats down and dives in.

That sure feels different! *Now* I understand! I get out of the pool and dive right back in.

Beside the pool, there's a bathhouse with a side for the ladies and a side for the men. One day when I have to go to the bathroom there is a lady changing her clothes in there. I walk in and she isn't wearing anything. I'm so embarrassed I pretend I didn't see her, but mostly I'm scared. I never saw a grown-up lady without her clothes on before. I can't wait to get out of there. I don't want to ever look like that! She had giant brown nipples and hair on her bottom. I don't want that to happen to me. She was ugly and scary and I wonder if Mommy and other ladies are like that. I guess they must be. I don't want to be scary like that. I wish I never saw her.

At Spruce Lake, we sleep in a room with two double beds—one for Mommy and Daddy and one for me and Kelly. I hate sleeping with Kelly. We fight until we cry and Mommy won't let us talk to each other anymore. Kelly keeps getting on my side and she keeps pulling the covers away. I hate her.

When Baby Michelle is bigger, we bring a sleeping bag and a mat for someone to sleep on the floor. That someone is me! I like sleeping on the floor, and that way Michelle has to sleep with Kelly. I always make my bed on the floor beside Daddy—otherwise I can't sleep. Daddy snores as loud as a thunderstorm and I figured out that if I sleep beside him I can shake the bed with my leg and make him stop without getting up.

Another thing I love about Spruce Lake is the Snack Shop. It's wood like a cabin with wooden picnic tables inside and a counter where you can order anything! They have licorice and candy bars and popsicles and soft pretzels and hot dogs and slushies and everything you can think of. There is a Coke machine and a Pepsi machine. At home, we can't have Coke and Pepsi and 7UP, but here we can. We get to go there twice a day—once in the day and once in the night. Everybody goes there and eats and the kids play and the grown-ups talk.

My favorite part is at night when the yellow lights are on and you come inside and eat snacks, then when you go outside the woods are dark and you walk along the trail to your room and you hear the crickets singing and you hear the people talking behind you and you know you get to come back tomorrow.

In the summer time, Mommy sometimes takes us to Manheim Pool instead of swimming in the pond. I like the pool because you can jump in and because you can see the bottom. Also, there's no mud to make your toes orange.

Mommy doesn't like Manheim Pool very much because they have a loudspeaker there and they play rock music. Rock music is from the devil and we shouldn't listen to it. But we can't help it if we're swimming and it's on the loudspeaker. I tell Mommy that it's ok because we aren't paying attention to the music, we're playing. Mommy says it doesn't matter; if we hear those songs over and over, they get into our minds. They play rock music on the bus too, but I don't say that to Mommy. What if she won't let us get on the bus anymore?

Mommy finds out about Pinch Pond and she starts taking us there instead. Pinch Pond isn't a pond—it's a pool and there's nothing about pinching. It's littler than Manheim Pool, but there aren't as many people and it has grass around it, not just cement. It doesn't have any music and we like it the same as Manheim Pool. The only thing we care about at the pool is staying a long, long time!

Mommy decides to make our swimming suits. She doesn't like the pretty ones they make for little girls. We like them, but she doesn't. They aren't even real swimming suits. She buys fuzzy red material and they have two parts, but not like a two-piece where your belly is out like Karen has. Mommy says God wants us to cover our bellies.

Our new swimming suits have a shirt without sleeves and bloomers. The good thing about them is it's kind of like wearing shorts, but otherwise I think they're dumb. Everybody looks at us funny and says, "Is that your pajamas? Why don't you wear a swimming suit?" We say, "This *is* our swimming suit." Then they ask why and we have to say our mom made it and we have to wear it. They ask why again. We say we don't know.

Mommy says it's because real swimming suits are immodest and we shouldn't show off our bodies like that. We say we aren't showing off, we're just swimming. When Mommy gets tired of us, she says, "Because that's just the way we do it at our house," and that's the end.

Daddy decides we can have sheep because there aren't any animals in the barn now. When I was little there used to be steers and pigs in there, but not anymore. Daddy built a hog house so he can have lots of pigs, and he doesn't like steers. He likes sheep, though, so he gets 30. I like the sheep, but they don't like me. They don't like any people except Daddy because Daddy feeds them. He calls them, "Here Shippy Shippy Shippy," and they all run up to him and walk after him. All our sheep are white, but Daddy wants a black one too. He buys a black one and names her Hagar because there's a black lady in the Bible and her name is Hagar.

In the summer, the sheep live in the meadow. In the winter, they live in the barn. Then they learn to know us and they don't run away anymore when we come close to them. All the sheep are girls except Jake and in the spring we have lots of babies! Sheep have twins a lot and sometimes they have triplets. I pick one of the babies to be especially mine. Daddy tells me to pick a girl because the boys are all going to market. I pick a nice one that has two little spots on her face that look like eyes. I name her Four Eyes. When I tell my friends at school that I have a lamb named Four Eyes everyone laughs and tells me that's a dumb name. Well, it's too late now and I don't really care and neither does Four Eyes.

When it starts to get hot, the shearing men come and shear the sheep. They each take a turn getting caught and having all their wool shaved off. They hate that even though they must feel better without their winter coats. After they get sheared, they look like they don't have any clothes on and they run around and seem confused.

Roger Bridges comes to our house and lives in the spare room. He's going to be like our brother and I'm so excited because I always wanted a big brother. Roger is 16 and he doesn't have to go to school anymore if he lives on a farm and helps Daddy.

Roger is adopted and he is very bad! He doesn't listen to his mommy and daddy who adopted him and he doesn't go to school and he steals things and had to go to jail. But he can't stay in jail because he's only a boy so he comes to our house. I never knew a real bad boy before who said swear words and lied and stole and wouldn't listen.

I like Roger. Me and Roger are friends. We help Daddy together when I don't have to go to school because I always help Daddy. I don't like staying in the house.

Me and Roger both like going fishing. Now I don't have to wait for Daddy—I can go with Roger. I hope Roger can be my big brother forever. Our favorite thing to do, me and Roger, is get up at five o'clock in the morning when it's still cold and wet out and go fishing for our breakfast. We catch sunnies and Roger cleans them and Mommy fries them in the garage in the electric frying pan because she hates fish. I love them—especially getting up early to catch them with Roger. We go fishing all the time. Sometimes we tell stories and sometimes we just stand there.

Roger tells me about the orphanage where he stayed when he was little. He said the big boys beat up the little boys and there was no one there to make them stop it. He said that they ate macaroni and cheese out of a big pot, all of them, and the big mean boys got it all. He told me his mommy and daddy didn't want him. They gave him away to an orphanage, and his sisters Brenda and Cecilia too. Roger told me one day his mommy was sewing on the sewing machine and his daddy came up behind her and made her sew her

180

finger. Poor Roger. His mommy and daddy didn't love God and they didn't love him either. I love him. I want him to stay with us until we all grow up.

Then Roger has to leave because summer comes and we're going to Montana. I want him to come too, but Mommy and Daddy say *No*. He goes back to live with Earl Bridges and Melba, who adopted him and Brenda and Cecilia. I don't know what to do without Roger. I don't go fishing much anymore after that. I don't feel like it without Roger.

I'm in third grade when Aunt Barbie goes to Africa. Aunt Barbie is Daddy's sister and she didn't get married. Aunt Barbie is a teacher and I want to be a teacher too when I grow up. Aunt Barbie goes to Africa to be a missionary for three years. I can't believe we won't see her for *three years*. That is a really long time.

When she comes back, I'll be big. I'll be in sixth grade. After sixth grade is seventh and I can't even imagine being *that* big! When Aunt Barbie comes back, I'll know how to do hard math problems and read hard books and I'll be tall and pretty.

Me and Kelly catch a snapping turtle. We are walking in the lane after school and we find it there. I never saw a snapping turtle before, but I know what it is because Daddy told us about them. This is the biggest turtle I ever saw, and Kelly too. It has a beak like a bird and it has pointy things on its shell and on its tail. Daddy says snapping turtles are like dinosaurs—that's how I know this one is a snapping turtle.

Daddy sets traps to catch snapping turtles so they don't eat the ducks. This one stops walking when we get to it. I think we should catch it for Daddy, but I know we can't touch it.

If a snapping turtle bites you, it won't ever let go until you chop its head off. But we don't have anything to put it in. It's too big to fit into our book bags, plus it might get out and bite us. We need a box. We don't have any boxes now, but there are some in the garage. I don't think we can make that turtle walk into the box and we better not push it even with our shoes. We need a shovel too—a big one. I tell Kelly to stay there with the turtle; I'm going to get a box and a shovel from the garage. If it tries to get away, she can scare it and it will go back inside its shell. I have to hurry because if someone comes to our house, they might run over it.

I go into the garage real quiet so that Mommy won't hear me. If I tell her, we need a shovel and a box to catch a turtle, Mommy will know it isn't a regular turtle and she'll make us leave it alone.

Mommy doesn't hear me.

That turtle is very heavy. He scratches around, but he can't get out of the box. When we get to the house, we yell, "Mommy, Mommy, look! We caught a snapping turtle."

Mommy says, "Oh, for crying out loud! I wondered what you girls were doing! You be careful with that thing!"

Daddy is even more surprised than Mommy and he thinks it's very funny that we got a box and a shovel to catch it with. He tells us we did a good job, but next time we see a snapping turtle, better just leave it alone.

In school, I'm smart. I'm not that smart in math, but I'm smart in everything else. I'm especially smart in reading and I get to be in the top reading group with Neil, who is so smart he's even smart in math.

Me and Neil get picked to go to LEAP class. LEAP is a special class that the smart kids from all the schools get to go to once a week. We do fun things in LEAP like make things and do puzzles and play games and do projects. I love LEAP. LEAP doesn't have any tests or homework or spelling words (which I'm not very good at), it's just fun games for the smart kids.

But when we go to LEAP class me and Neil miss regular school. The other kids make fun of us and say, "LEAP Class! LEAP Class!" And they jump up and down and ask us if we play leap frog. I don't like when they do that because LEAP class is fun and we *don't* play leap frog. I think they're just jealous that me and Neil get to miss school and don't get in trouble. And they know it's because we're the smartest.

Sometimes I get ready for school really fast and so I can walk to the bus stop in the morning. I don't do it much because it's special. Also, you have to be careful or you could miss the bus. And I always walk by myself; Kelly isn't ready and Mommy has to take her in the car later like normal.

I walk out the lane and up the big hill and the air is still so cool I have to wear my jacket. The grass is still wet and the sky is hazy. My lunchbox is heavy and clunks against my leg. I feel big and brave walking all by myself. Everything is quiet and sometimes I get to the bus stop first before everyone else.

A fter the news, *Little House on the Prairie* comes on and we're allowed to watch it. There's Ma and Pa and Laura and Mary and Carrie and there's Mr. Edwards and the Olson's. The Olson family is funny, especially Harriet and Nellie. They're mean to everybody, but they're funny.

Laura's family is like our family, with three girls. I'm like Laura and Kelly's like Mary and Michelle is like Carrie. I'm like Laura because Laura likes to do a lot of things and she helps her daddy and she isn't scared of anything. Laura is bad a lot like me. She looks like me too. Kelly is like Mary because Mary is always good and so is Kelly. Michelle is like Carrie because she's the littlest. In *Little House on the Prairie*, Mary is the oldest and Laura comes next. In our family, I'm the biggest and then comes Kelly, but I'm still more like Laura and not like Mary at all. Mary likes to help in the house and so does Kelly. Not me.

Sometimes something bad comes on and Mommy and Daddy have to turn it off. They turn it off if something is burning down or if there's a wagon accident or if someone is dying or doing something bad like hurting people. They say, "We don't need to watch this," and they turn it off. They don't want us to have bad dreams or see bad people.

Little House on the Prairie is a lot like us. Ma makes dresses for Laura and Mary like the dresses Mommy makes for us. They can't wear pants either, not even in the winter, and not even culotte skirts. Their Pa goes hunting like Daddy and has a farm. Ma takes care of the house and them like Mommy. We even have the same hair because they have to have long hair and pigtails too. But we don't have any neighbors like Mrs. Olson.

Me and Kelly are walking home from the bus stop and we see the geese. They are eating the grass beside the lane, close to the house. We keep walking, but they don't move. They stand right there and keep eating. We know they are waiting for us because we have to walk past them and they will get us.

We stop walking. We decide we could trick the geese. We could go around the pond and past the chicken houses and even up behind the barn if we have to. Ha ha! We're smarter than those dumb old geese! It's a long way around the pond, but we can do it.

We go all the way around and when we get out of the meadow and onto the other lane by the chicken houses, we see what the geese did. They changed their minds and are walking around the other way coming right toward us. I know they want to get us. They are smarter than we thought.

Me and Kelly hurry up and we go inside House 2. We can see those horrible mean geese right outside the door. Then I remember House 2 has a telephone and I can reach it if I stand on a bucket. I know how you call Mommy because Daddy does it when he's tending the chickens. You dial the number and then hang up. First the phone starts ringing and then when it stops ringing you pick it up and the other person is saying, "Hello? Hello?"

Mommy is saying "Hello?" when I pick it up. She is *very* surprised it's me calling! I tell her me and Kelly are in House 2 and the geese won't let us out. She comes out to the chicken house and throws stones at the geese to chase them away so we can come out. We are very hungry for our snack!

The barn is full of pigeons and I love them. Daddy says they're dirty birds like rats, but they are not. They're all colors of black and white and gray and tan and brown with pretty sparkly green and purple parts on their wings. They say, "Prrrrr-Prrrrr" when you walk into the barn quietly and they fly away if you make a lot of noise. If you throw corn on the ground, they come eat it. I like their tiny heads and little eyes. I want to pet them, but no matter how nice I am they won't let me.

I tell Daddy to please catch me one, but he says "No."

I say please so many times he finally says, "Okay."

I make a nice home in the old fox pen. It's big enough that I can go inside. Daddy catches me a bunch of pigeons and I name them all.

Something terrible happens to the pigeons, even worse than what happened to the ducks. The pigeons don't like me. They don't get used to me like the sheep. They don't care if I feed them and talk nice to them. When I go outside to play, Mommy makes me feed them. She asks me, "Did you check your pigeons?" and I say "yes" even when I didn't. Those stupid pigeons don't like me, but if they were hungry they would be happy when they saw me coming.

Then when I do go to check them they're all dead. It's my fault they're dead because I didn't feed them and I said I did. I didn't mean to kill them. I didn't think they would die that fast.

I think about those poor pigeons starving to death in their cage because they were scared of me. That wasn't fair. I should have let them out instead. I feel something terrible in my belly and I know I did something really bad. It wasn't exactly an accident like the duckies when I was little.

When I tell Mommy and Daddy, they say, "They must have gotten a disease," and I don't get into trouble. But I know they didn't. I should have gotten spanked.

I never ever tell anyone what a bad thing I did, but I have bad dreams about it all my life.

I want to play kickball. Only the boys play kickball, but I want to play. I can kick. So I tell them and they have to let me because everyone can play what they want at recess. Most of the boys can kick and throw better than me, but other boys get picked even more last than me. Sometimes I miss but sometimes I kick it really hard.

Jeremy wants to kick the ball for me and then I can run. He can kick really hard and that way our team can win. I say, "No." I tell him, "How am I supposed to learn to kick the ball if I never do?" I want to kick it. Besides, that's the fun part. That's why it's *kickball*. If I don't kick it very good, too bad.

B oth my Grandmas and Grandpas live on farms like us. Grandpa Zimmerman has chicken houses like Daddy's. He has old chicken houses too that they don't use anymore. The old ones have windows so that the chickens can see out. Grandpa Brubaker has a barn with steers and a big stone water trough for them that has a spigot running into it. We have to be careful because there's a wire there to keep the steers from jumping out and if you touch it, it will shock you.

Grandma Zimmerman's house is big and I like it because it has a porch that goes all the way around. In the summer, me and Doris play on the porch while the aunts make dinner and the uncles sit out there with the fan on. My favorite thing about Grandma Zimmerman's house is the stairway. It has a banister like the kind you slide down, but I can't slide down it because I'm not allowed. I could try it when no one is looking, but if I fall down, I will break Grandma's lamp and make a lot of noise and get into big trouble. Grandma Zimmerman has a sofa in the kitchen. Not too many people have a sofa in their kitchen and I think that's a good idea.

Grandma Brubaker's house is very big and very old. They have another house too and that one is called the Tenant House. Mommy says that when she was little they lived in the Tenant House. Now other people live in the Tenant House and Grandma and Grandpa live in the big house. It has a lot of windows. Downstairs is Grandpa's office and the laundry and the kitchen and the dining room and the family room and the living room. The living room is big and cold. We go in there when it's Christmas and all the cousins come.

We don't even know what all is upstairs. It's so big we aren't allowed to go into all the rooms. We can go into Mommy's old room and Aunt Lucy's old room, but on the other side, there's a door and we aren't allowed to go in there. I don't know why. Mommy says there's nothing in there and we don't need to go in there. But I want to see in.

Mommy says, "That's Uncle Roy's old room and there's nothing in there for little girls to play with."

Sometimes we get to see in there when Mommy or Grandma go in. There are rooms that have other rooms attached to them and I think I could get lost if I go in there by myself. There's another stairway going down and I ask Mommy where it goes. She says it goes into the dining room where we play Church on the steps.

Oh. That's funny—a stairway into the dining room. I didn't know that door went somewhere upstairs.

Then Grandma and Grandpa Brubaker get old too and sell their farm to somebody else. I'm sad because I like that house. It has big windowsills and a dinner bell and two porches and a real water pump outside. Mommy lived there when she was little and all the Brubakers lived there since they made Pennsylvania. Now we can't go there anymore. We can, but somebody else lives there.

Grandma and Grandpa move to a new house with Grandpa's desk and the grandfather clock and the living room chairs and all the same dollies and the same yellow bedspread with bumps on it. But I wish they still lived in the old house with the cuckoo clock and the big stairway and all the secret places. All my life I dream about that big house.

Something very scary happens. There's a place near us called "TMI," which means Three Mile Island, and something bad happens there. That's where they make electricity, and some radiation gets out in a big bubble and if the bubble pops we have to leave or we're going to die. Everybody is very scared. We don't have to go to school and we can't go outside. Mommy and Daddy say God is taking care of us so we shouldn't worry, but nobody knows what's going to happen.

Daddy calls Uncle Paul, who lives far away from TMI, and asks him if we can go to his house if the bubble pops. Uncle Paul says yes, so we pack our suitcases in case the people on the radio tell us we should leave. I like going to stay overnight at other people's houses, but if we have to go this time, it's going to be because something very bad happened.

Daddy says that if the bubble pops we won't hear it or see it but that the air will be dangerous and that people and animals and plants will get sick and maybe die. I look out the window and think about the things that might die: the kitties will die and the dogs will die and the chickens and the pigs and the flowers and trees and the corn. I ask Daddy if the fish in the pond will die and he says, "They might."

I want to take Fancy and Pooch, but we can't. I ask if I can take the bucket of minnows I got from the pond. I'm not allowed. I look at those little minnows and I hope the bubble doesn't burst so they can grow into fish and everything will be alright.

I ask Daddy how long we have to stay at Uncle Paul's. He doesn't know. What if we have to move far far away and never come back? I

194

wonder whose house Grandma is going to, and Kristen and Katrina and Tommy and Darvin.

The men fix TMI and we don't have to go anywhere. We can put our suitcases away and go to school again. I'm glad everything's going to be ok, but it's too bad we didn't get to go to Uncle Paul's for at least one night.

When I'm nine, Mommy and Daddy say I'm big enough to learn to ice skate. It's cold and the pond is frozen like a rock. Daddy goes down there and jumps on it really hard. If it doesn't break *then*, it's very strong and no one can break it.

Sometimes you can see down through the ice and it's a little scary. You feel like you could fall in and die even though Daddy said it's okay. The ice has cracks. Daddy says the cracks are good cracks because the pond has to crack when it freezes. If there aren't any cracks, then you better be careful! Even though the cracks are good cracks, they still look dangerous.

Mommy helps me learn to skate. I have to be careful because the ice skates are sharp like knives and you could cut yourself or somebody else.

Ice skating is hard!! I stand up on my skates and fall right down! Mommy helps me get up but as soon as I start to go I fall down again and Mommy falls down too. We land on our bottoms on the hard ice and say, "OWWW!" and laugh. Skating is fun because it feels like you're flying, but I fall a lot. I go skating every day and I fall so much Daddy says I should put a pillow in my snow pants for my bottom. I would do it, but it won't fit. I fall over so much that I hurt my wrists and I have to wear Ace bandages like I broke them. I keep skating, though, because I like going fast and I want to learn to do it good like Mommy.

In the winter, we can wear pants like other people unless we're going to church or to Grandma's or Aunt Judy's. When it isn't cold, we have to wear dresses or skirts or culoutte skirts. I like culotte skirts the best because they have legs in them and I can sit any way I want. In regular dresses, you have to sit nice. Mommy makes us culoutte skirts with flaps so that they look like a regular skirt. There's a square of material in the middle of the front and in the middle of the back so you can't see it's a skirt with legs. Mommy likes us to wear that kind more.

Everybody at school asks us what the flaps are for. They laugh at me and ask me if they're towels. They're *not* towels, they're flaps and I don't know why I have to wear them, but I do. I ask Mommy if she could make me culoutte skirts without flaps, but Mommy says, "No." Mommy says the flap kind are more modest and it's important for girls to be modest.

I know the Devil makes people laugh at us for following Jesus and we shouldn't worry about them. But I don't think Jesus cares about flaps—I think Mommy is making them up. The flaps are dumb. I want to be a good girl and do what's right, but I don't understand. You can still tell it's a culotte skirt. You can still tell I have two legs.

Mommy and Daddy take us to see a play about a girl named Helen Keller. We have to sit and be quiet like in church, but this is fun. A play is at nighttime, like Bible School or Prayer Meeting, and when it's time to start they turn the lights off and it's very dark.

Helen Keller is a little girl who can't see or hear. She is very very naughty and no one can make her be good because she can't see her mommy and she can't hear her saying, "No." Helen smacks and pinches and kicks. She screams. She can't talk because no one can teach her. Then a special teacher comes and she helps Helen Keller to learn and understand.

I liked it best when Helen Keller was naughty. That was funny. Me and Kelly's favorite part was when Helen was eating. She didn't know about spoons and she didn't know about your own plate so she reached around with her hands and ate off everyone's plates and spilled the water.

Now when me and Kelly are messy or noisy at the table or reach for things or want something each other is eating, Mommy calls us Helen Keller. I bet Helen Keller had to wear diapers even when she was a big girl until that teacher taught her about going to the bathroom.

I like reading books and writing stories. Sometimes in church when the preacher is preaching I write little stories on my pretty tablet. We aren't allowed to read in church because everyone would be able to see we aren't listening. Mommy lets me write, though, because if you're writing, you might be writing about what the preacher is saying. I make up a person to be besides me and then I pretend I'm them and write a story. It's fun. I am not listening or writing about the preacher or Jesus or God. But Mommy doesn't know that.

I read a book called *Harriet the Spy* and I like it so much I read it again even though I already know what happens. Harriet is a little girl like me. She decides to be a spy so she gets a notebook and writes down everything everyone is doing. She lives in the city, so she even has neighbors she can spy on and write down what they are doing.

We don't have any neighbors. I can only spy on Kelly and Michelle and Mommy and Daddy. I spy on Kelly and Michelle and write on my tablet what dumb things they are playing.

Harriet also writes other things in her spy book. She writes what she thinks about too—sometimes nice things and sometimes mean things. Sometimes she writes things she can't ever say because if she did, she would get into big trouble. I try it. I know you shouldn't say some things, but if you write them down, nobody will ever know. And then you kind of feel like you said it but you aren't in trouble.

I get a great idea. I ask Mommy if I can have a real notebook because I'm going to make a diary. I don't have to spy on anybody. I can write down whatever I want to and when I'm big I will be able to read it. Then I can remember what it is like to be little when I'm big. If I have a little girl who wants to take gymnastics or play the drums or if she smacks her sister for eating her candy bar, I'll remember that she isn't trying to be bad. And when I'm an old lady I can read all about my whole life starting from when I was nine and see if I forgot anything.

Mommy smiles and says, "Yes." She gives me a red notebook that I can write anything I want to in. I write about how all the girls got sick and had to stay home from church. If I put something in it every day and never stop, it will be like writing a very big book about me. I'm going to try it.

March 9, 1980

Today is Sunday and all the girls are sick. Mommy, Yvonne, Wanda and me stayed home from church. Only Daddy and Roger went. I was absent from school all week with fever, headache, sneezing, coughing and I threw up once so far. I had a fever of 101.8 then 100. We have six lambs—Freckles, Speckles, Hobbles, Wobbles, Spot and Dot. I would LOVE to have a horse, but Daddy says we have only 90 dollars in savings. I just got this notebook today. I am nine and four months. Our president is Jimmy Carter. The government is Dick Thornburg. It is 9:15 PM. Good night.